TO

_____

FROM

_____

DATE

_____

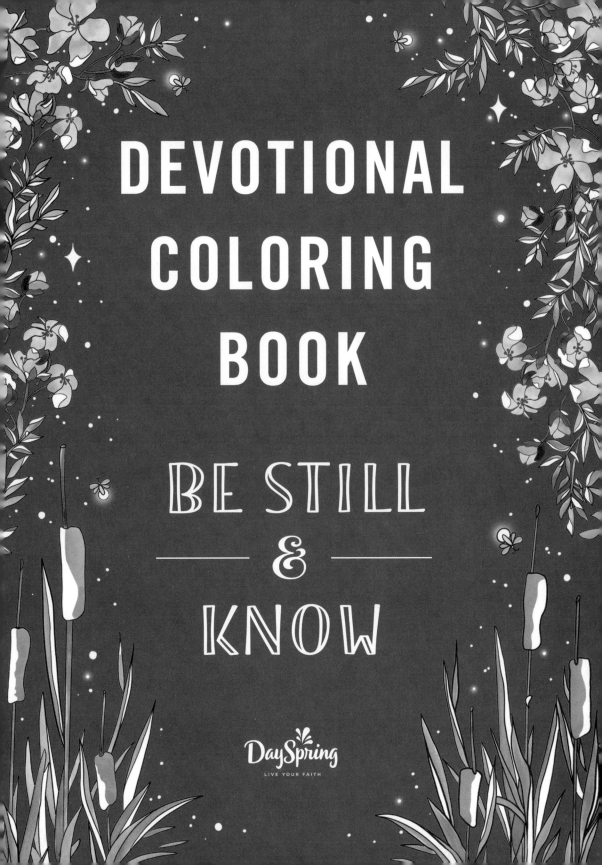

Be Still & Know: Devotional Coloring Book
Copyright © 2023 DaySpring. All rights reserved.
First Edition, June 2023

Published by:

21154 Highway 16 East
Siloam Springs, AR 72761
dayspring.com

Cover Design by: Kelley Brady
Illustrations by: Kelley Brady, Jon Huckeby, Jenna Wilusz

Printed in Vietnam
Prime: J9592
ISBN: 978-1-64870-917-3

Time after time throughout all of Scripture, God invites us to rest from our busy lives and to be still in His presence. He invites us to remember that He alone is in charge and has a plan bigger that is better than ours. He, the All-Powerful One, is God . . . and we are not.

When we remember this fundamental truth, two miracles unfold. First, we find delightful freedom. It is amazing how light our hearts feel when we know that someone stronger and more capable than us shoulders our burdens. Then, as we witness His faithfulness in our struggles, we find our souls able to settle into true trust. Surrender to and trust in our more-than-capable and loving Father as He ushers us into lasting peace and promised rest.

This *Devotional Coloring Book* is a seventy-seven-day sabbatical. As you read these devotions and fill in the coloring pages, allow God's presence to calm your mind and open your soul to the messages of hope in each devotion.

Read, color, pray, and breathe in His goodness.

A DAY OF REST

Then He said to them,
"The Sabbath was made for man,
not man for the Sabbath."

MARK 2:27 NIV

As Jesus and His hungry disciples passed through a grain field, they picked heads of grain to eat along the way. Now, according to Deuteronomy 23:25, it was lawful to pick heads of grain by hand from a man's grain field, but the Pharisees demanded to know why they were "working" on the Sabbath. "Six days you shall do your work, but on the seventh day you shall rest; that your ox and your donkey may have rest, and the son of your servant woman, and the alien, may be refreshed" (Exodus 23:12 ESV). The law of Moses (Deuteronomy 5:14) commanded them to keep the Sabbath, but the question was "how" to keep it. The Jews added a burdensome number of man-made laws designed toward this end.

But as usual, Jesus had a response that cut to the truth and skipped the superficial blame game. He reminded the Pharisees that David and his men, who were also hungry in their flight from King Saul, ate the showbread, which only priests were allowed to eat. Sure, David technically broke the law of Moses. But under certain conditions of need, Jesus demonstrated that the violation was allowable. The true needs of humankind were more important than following religion to the letter. God created the Sabbath as a day of rest from their toil. The Sabbath day is meant to be a blessing to us, a time of rest and restoration, and a day to worship and rejoice in the Lord, who made us.

FATHER, THANK YOU FOR BEING LORD OVER EVEN THE SABBATH. THANK YOU FOR DESIGNING US FOR REST. TEACH ME TO HONOR YOUR DESIGN FOR MY LIFE, AND TO TRULY REST.

THE HURRIER I GET

Careful planning puts you ahead in the long run;
hurry and scurry put you further behind.

PROVERBS 21:5 THE MESSAGE

The apostle Paul was a get-up-and-go kind of guy. He shared the gospel in at least fifty cities and would likely have continued sharing if he had not been imprisoned. The energetic apostle must have wondered what possible good he could do stuck behind bars, yet in those quiet hours, he was able to sit down and write his letters to the church. In the stillness of a sedentary life, Paul completed what God wanted him to accomplish, though he would likely never have imagined his sentence to be God's will for his life.

Like Paul, most of us have our ideas of what life should look like. We've got priorities, goals, and obligations. We're all in a hurry. Our employers sometimes breathe down our necks to rush an important project through too quickly, often with poor results—proving the adage that there's never enough time to do it right the first time but always enough time to do it over again. If the internet lags, or our food gets delayed at a restaurant, or traffic is a little heavier than we expected—well, our temper or our mood may come into question.

In this age of instant everything, it is hard not to interpret God's delays as denials. We want what we want when we want it! Yet the discipline of delay is another expression of God's love for us. His timing is perfect. Every. Single. Time. He's never early and never, ever late. But learning to believe that about Him in the moment is truly a sign of maturity in Him. The more we learn to lean into His promise to provide what we need, when we need it, the more peace we will carry deep inside of us.

FATHER, GIVE ME PEACE AS I LEARN TO TRUST IN YOUR TIMING. I BELIEVE YOU GET IT RIGHT, EVERY SINGLE TIME.

GREEN PASTURES IN THE PRESENT

The LORD is my shepherd, I lack nothing.
He makes me lie down in green pastures,
He leads me beside quiet waters, He refreshes my soul.

PSALM 23:1–3 NIV

That familiar feeling of panic is about to set in, and you feel it rising from the pit of your stomach straight to your head. As if on steroids, your mind races ahead of the emotion, rehearsing all the details that must be done or fall into place before you can finally get a grip. In the moment (and it turns out there are many of these moments every day), it feels like so much is at stake if you fail. Fear grips you and threatens to sabotage your plans, your work—and ultimately your worth.

But as always, fear is a liar. If you are God's child, you are not on your own, struggling to pull all the necessary strings to make life work in your favor. With Jesus at your side, you lack nothing! His all-powerful hand leads you through life's twists and turns, always providing access to the calm, gentle streams of His indwelling Spirit. No matter how crazy the day gets, God's presence with you in it is a verdant pasture of peace for your soul.

Today, if you feel panicked about an upcoming project or problem, don't let your mind race with all the what-ifs. Instead, put your mind and heart to rest by remembering that your God has this day—and your life—in His hands. Let the Shepherd lead you through each moment as you acknowledge His presence and goodness in it. Look to Him for guidance and lie down in His promised care.

LORD, MY SHEPHERD, RESTING IN YOU IS THE VERY BEST PLACE TO BE. I WILL SEEK WAYS TO FIND COMFORT IN YOUR SHADOW TODAY. SHOW ME THE WAY.

SAILING STONES

*You yourselves like living stones are being built up
as a spiritual house, to be a holy priesthood,
to offer spiritual sacrifices acceptable to God through Jesus Christ.*

I PETER 2:5 ESV

If you've ever heard the expression "A rolling stone gathers no moss," then you will probably understand the concept of "sailing stones" found in a remote area of Death Valley, California. These heavy stones etch long tracks behind them across a dried lakebed known as Racetrack Playa. The stones, which range in size from several ounces to hundreds of pounds, seem to travel along the desert ground without human or animal intervention. No one has ever claimed to have actually seen them move, but the trails behind the stones seem to suggest that they do indeed move. In 2014 scientists were able to capture the stones' movements using time-lapse photography. What the camera revealed was a propelling force of ice, water, and wind. Rains would collect, freezing overnight to create a slick surface that would thaw the next day. Winds would then break down the ice sheet, melting, with the effect of propelling the stones forward across the lakebed.

"A rolling stone gathers no moss" is a proverb with a bit of advice for people who cannot seem to settle in one place for long. Lichens and mosses grow slowly in stable environments, never on rolling stones. Some people sail through life because they fear settling in one place for too long, or staying with a job or in a relationship, often avoiding responsibilities and the cares of everyday life. But fear and faith are as incompatible as rolling stones and moss. Trusting in God, the Rock of your salvation, is the right move.

FATHER, MAKE ME A STONE THAT SETTLES IN YOU AND YOU ALONE. I TRUST YOU TO DO WITH MY LIFE WHAT YOU HAVE PURPOSED FOR ME.

A TIME TO SIT AND THINK

Relax, everything's going to be all right;
rest, everything's coming together;
open your hearts, love is on the way!

JUDE 2 THE MESSAGE

God's best is always grounded in love, and it's always what He wants for our lives: the best next step; the best path to our growth; the best outcome. We all have days when the waves crash relentlessly, and our beach bag, filled with everything we thought we needed, goes floating out to sea. We sit silent, soaking wet and feeling helpless. Those are the days when the deeper breaths are needed, the fearless faith is tested, and the blind trust that everything is coming together for our good is more important than the overwhelming circumstances in front of us. Especially when it looks like the circumstances have washed away all our hopes and dreams.

Grace sufficient to handle each day comes in twenty-four-hour increments. We have what we need when we need it. Every day will move us toward a place where we exercise more trust, enjoy more peace, and look a little more like Jesus. That's all that really matters because that's all that's eternally measured—what we do to point others to Him.

Some things we pack in our "survival" bags from day-to-day weigh us down and slow our progress. God allows the washing away of dependencies we hold too tightly, self-security we lean on too much, and material things distracting us too often. He wants us to rest in Him just like we relax into a day at the beach: a time to sit and think about the magnitude of His love, the never-ending waves of His grace, and His thoughts of us that outnumber the grains of sand. He doesn't rest while caring for every detail of our lives. That frees us to rest in knowing everything's coming together for good—with an ocean of love behind it.

FATHER, I'M RELAXED IN YOUR LOVING CARE TODAY.

LIVE TOTALLY SURRENDERED

Trust in the LORD with all your heart and lean not
on your own understanding; in all your ways submit to him,
and he will make your paths straight.

PROVERBS 3:5–6 NIV

In 1888, Dora Yu entered medical school at age fifteen. When she graduated, she offered her diploma to God. As a doctor, she healed many even though she was afflicted with her own infirmity. As an entrepreneur, she started a girls' school and a church. As an evangelist, she led hundreds of people into a relationship with Christ.

Dora lived a life of total surrender. She embodied prayer without ceasing, engaging in perpetual conversation with God throughout her day. She prayed that God would keep her in total obedience, total surrender, and total compassion. More than anything, she wanted her life to reflect Christ's; she wanted to love others unconditionally. She longed to see the world from God's viewpoint and live in the heavenly realm.

Colossians 4:2–4 says, "Continue steadfastly in prayer, being watchful in it with thanksgiving. At the same time, pray also for us, that God may open to us a door for the word, to declare the mystery of Christ . . . that I may make it clear, which is how I ought to speak" (ESV). Dora understood that she had to remain prayerful if she wanted to impact the world for Christ. She knew that a life of prayerlessness was a sign of pride and self-reliance. More than anything, she knew she needed God.

If you lived a life of constant prayer, how might your life change?

True surrender leads us out of our comfort zones and into God's plan and will. When we completely surrender to the Lord, God might ask us to change jobs or move to a different location. But one thing is for sure: being totally surrendered to God brings major world change.

DEAR GOD, FORGIVE ME FOR THE HOURS AND DAYS WHEN I NEGLECT TO INCLUDE YOU IN MY LIFE. I WANT TO SPEND MORE TIME WITH YOU. HELP ME DEVELOP A HEALTHY HABIT OF REGULARLY TALKING WITH YOU AND SURRENDERING MY WILL TO YOURS.

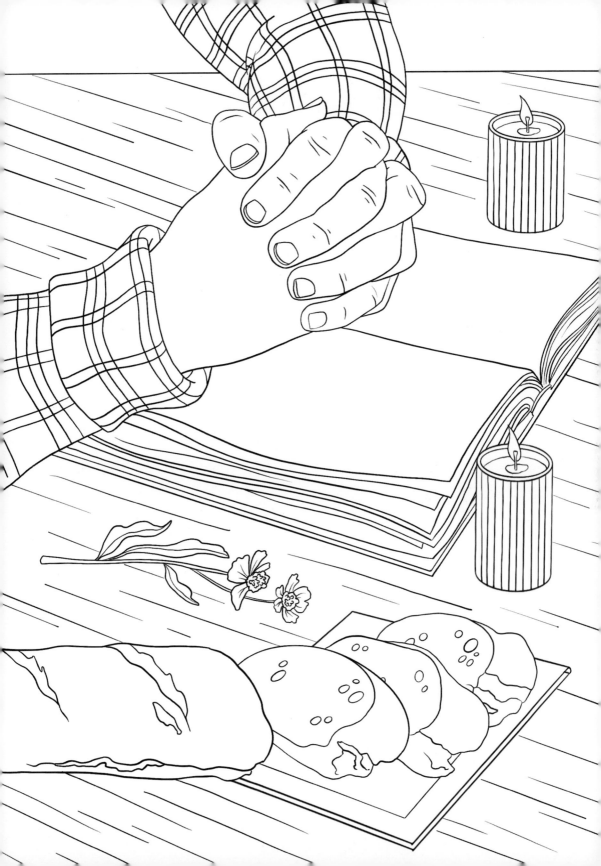

MOVING TOWARD A QUIET TRUST

Teach me, and I will be quiet; show me where I have been wrong.

JOB 6:24 NIV

God created us and put us on this earth to realize how miraculously we're made, and to discover that a simple life is anchored in a simple truth. God loves us too much to let us go. *Ever.* It doesn't matter if we get it all wrong some days. When we rush past opportunities to listen, to rest, to pray, to stop and get directions, there's a good chance we'll get a whole bunch of things wrong. But grace is patient, certain, and steadying.

Every day is another chance to push away from the chaos. When we get entangled in the idea that we must accomplish a set number of tasks or prove our worth by the world's measure of success, we risk never being able to slow down and learn how to simply be quiet. It's a discipline we'll master only by asking for God's help. He sees the things we can't see. He's written our days. He wants us to remember how sufficient He is and how infinitely He cares. It's up to us to quiet the noisy demands in our heads, the loud expectations we've put on ourselves, and the nagging impossibility of perfection—in our homes, our jobs, our families, and our social media posts.

Maybe we can start our days in a different way. Our eyes open with a quiet thank-You. Our first deep breath brings a quiet smile. A healthy stretch from head to toe releases our hours into God's hands. There is nothing more comforting or faithful than His care. It's as relentless as our list of things to do, but He can be trusted with what gets done—and what doesn't. Remember the moments that make up the minutes belong to the One who's teaching us to simply trust.

> DEAR GOD, QUIET MY HEART TO HEAR YOUR VOICE, LEARN TO TRUST, AND LET GO OF THE PRESSURES CONTROLLING MY DAY. I GIVE IT ALL TO YOU AND THE PEACE OF YOUR CARE.

BROKEN TO BEAUTIFUL

*I want you to know that through Jesus
the forgiveness of sins is proclaimed to you.*

ACTS 13:38 NIV

If you break your favorite vase, no amount of glue will fix it completely. The crack may be difficult to see, but it will always be there. And the vessel will always be weaker than it was before the fall. Our relationship with God is also broken. There have been many human attempts to put the pieces back together, but our relationship with a holy God can't be mended—only replaced by something new.

Fortunately for us, that's exactly what God has in mind. He has made a way for us to enter into a new relationship with Him—forgiveness through His Son, Jesus. All we need to do to receive God's forgiveness is to acknowledge our need for it and ask Him for it. It's an act couched in simplicity, but it isn't necessarily easy. Our old sin nature doesn't want to examine the places in our hearts where we have failed. We have a hard time admitting our deep need for God. Pride lifts its ugly head, and the invitation goes unanswered. God is patient, however. As soon as you reach up to Him in humility, His hand is extended down to you in love. He loves you so much, and He greatly desires to walk in daily fellowship with you. Maybe you've already accepted His offer. If not, will you let Him replace your old, broken relationship with a brand-new one?

DEAR LORD, THANK YOU FOR LOVING ME THROUGH MY SHORTCOMINGS. WHERE YOU HAVE GIVEN ME A CLEAN SLATE AND A PURE HEART, I AM GRATEFUL. AND WHERE I NEED YOUR FORGIVENESS, I LAY DOWN MY LIFE ONCE AGAIN TO ASK FOR YOUR TENDER MERCY.

STRESS AND REST

Let all that I am wait quietly before God,
for my hope is in Him.

PSALM 62:5 NLT

Is there ever a time when you look around your desk, peruse your planner, or check your phone—shrug—and think, *Well, I guess there's nothing for me to do today*? Is there ever a moment when you can't think of anything that could use your attention? If you are a homeowner, then certainly not. If you are a mom, a teacher, a business owner, or a volunteer who cares for others, you are bombarded daily, if not more often. There is always something vying for your attention.

You inhabit an interconnected world that never slows down and never shuts off. The world tempts you to stay up late watching the news, or surfing the internet, or checking out social media, or gaming, or doing countless other activities that gobble up your time and distract you. But too much late-night screen time robs you of something you need very badly: sleep.

Are you going to bed at a reasonable hour and sleeping through the night? If so, you're both wise and blessed. But if you're staying up late with your eyes glued to a screen, overthinking problems, or getting one last thing done, then you're putting your long-term health at risk. And you're probably wasting time too. So the next time you're tempted to engage in wasting time late at night, resist the temptation. Instead, turn your thoughts and prayers to God. And when you're finished, turn off the lights and go to bed. You need rest.

LORD GOD, IT CAN BE SO DIFFICULT TO PRIORITIZE SLEEP! BUT I KNOW I NEED IT. PLEASE GENTLY REMIND ME TONIGHT THAT MY BODY NEEDS ITS RESTORATIVE REST.

WISDOM IN EIGHT WORDS

God wants His loved ones to get their proper rest.

PSALM 127:2 TLB

There's a popular Italian phrase—*dolce far niente*—which means "the art of doing nothing." Pleasant idleness. Not everyone understands how to properly rest. I think we like to stay on top of things and control as much of our lives and time as we can. And I admit it's a challenge for me to let go and let God. But if we're going to debate how to rest properly, we can't leave God out of it. As a matter of fact, He has to be the center of it, or we aren't going to enjoy any real rest.

God created our bodies to need rest. Endless health benefits come with releasing stress, disconnecting from work, and getting a good night's sleep. God wouldn't design us to need something that isn't found in Him. We're created in His image. We live and move and have our being in Him. But it's up to us to mentally and physically surrender to His perfect care. We've all been at the end of our day feeling exhausted and ready for bed, and as soon as we lie down, the thought reel starts rolling. This reel is never cued by God. We can't let that happen if we want the sweet sleep that He promises.

A few years ago, I met an elderly gentleman who gave me his advice for getting a good night's sleep. He told me he used the eight-after-eight routine every night. After 8 p.m., when it's time to start unwinding and think about going to bed, he prepared with eight words: *give it to God*

FATHER, TEACH ME THE ART OF DOING NOTHING. SWEET IDLENESS, IN YOUR WAY.

and go to sleep. He told me it had worked for him for as long as he could remember. I took it as good advice from a wise soul, and I've used it ever since.

THE LATTER AND THE FORMER RAIN

Fear the LORD our God, that giveth rain,
both the former and the latter, in His season.

JEREMIAH 5:24 KJV

Farmers know when a bad cloud comes up, they're fixing to have a gully washer. But the rains in Israel only came twice a year for farmers. Israel was not located near abundant sources of water like the Nile or the Euphrates, probably because God wanted them to depend solely on Him to provide all the water they needed. The former rains, or autumn rains, which fall October through November, are gentle showers that soften the ground for planting. But the latter are spring rains, March through April, and these rains come down harder and can cause flooding and destruction. But in James 5:7 we see the comparison of the former and latter rains to the Spirit of God: "Be patient, then, brothers and sisters, until the Lord's coming. See how the farmer waits for the land to yield its valuable crop, patiently waiting for the autumn and spring rains" (NIV). These rains represent God's provision and grace to us, just as the rains provided water for people, crops, and animals to survive throughout the year.

God has an abundance of blessings in store for us. He promises that He will pour out His Spirit on all flesh in the last days (Acts 2:17–21), an outpouring on all God's people from every nation and tongue. Just as the former rains prepared the land for seed and the latter rains for harvest, God will rain down His Spirit on us in the last days and bring in an abundance of souls to His glory.

FATHER, PATIENCE IS DIFFICULT FOR MANY OF US, BUT I BELIEVE YOUR PROMISE THAT PATIENCE IS A FRUIT GROWN BY THE HOLY SPIRIT. BLESS ME AS I GROW DEEPER INTO YOUR LOVE AND ABUNDANCE.

THE SOUND OF HIS VOICE

My child, pay attention to what I say.
Listen carefully to my words.

PROVERBS 4:20 NLT

In a noisy crowd, most of us can pick out the voice of our parent, spouse, or child. A mother, even though asleep, will wake up to the sound of her teenager coming home late at night. And many a video-watching office worker can detect the sound of the boss's footsteps coming from across the hall! Our ears are tuned to hear certain sounds, and we will strain forward to listen when we are trying to discern them.

As God enlivens the ears of your spirit, His voice is unmistakable. Even though you're surrounded by the clamor of a busy, noisy, and demanding world, you will hear His words of peace come through. Say you're lonely or sad or feel ashamed, and you find your voice to share your heart with Him through whispers in the middle of the night. Nevertheless, you will discern His tender words of assurance, forgiveness, and reconciliation. Suppose you'd like to live more openly and confidently as one of His own. Listen! His encouragement will come through, loud and clear!

God's ears are always fine-tuned to the sound of your voice. And it takes a lifetime of learning to hone your own ears to the vibrant sounds of His voice too. He wants that relationship with you, teaching you and speaking in ways that you delight to understand. The more you lean in, the more you discover the subtleties and unique aspects of His words to your spiritual ears. Listen close, and His voice will become the most beautiful thing you ever hear.

LORD, YOUR VOICE IS HONEY TO MY SOUL. PLEASE KEEP TEACHING ME TO HEAR YOU—AND TO RESPOND WITH JOY.

GARDEN GROWTH

The seed that fell on good soil represents those who truly hear and understand God's word and produce a harvest of thirty, sixty, or even a hundred times as much as had been planted!

MATTHEW 13:23 NLT

She led you through the halls of her humble home until she reached the back door, where she welcomed you to walk ahead. As you pushed open the door, it took a moment for your eyes to take in the beautiful scene before you. Nestled inside the old brick fence lining the perimeter of her property grew the most spectacular garden you had ever seen. A graceful weeping willow kept the corner guard, surrounded by dozens of daffodils standing at attention. Brilliant pink and red peonies, encore azaleas, and a variety of ferns and tall grasses lined the pebbled pathway. "What's your secret?" you wondered aloud as you inhaled the varied fragrances. Smiling, she answered, "The secret's in the soil."

Before she planted a single bulb, she tilled the soil, tested its quality, and added the right nutrients to create the perfect conditions for planting. But rooted in the right soil, beautiful growth was inevitable. Our hearts are much like our gardens. We may all hear the message of truth about God's grace and forgiveness, but only hearts that are tilled with humility and repentance receive those spiritual seeds. When we are open to receive God's grace, acknowledging our desperate need for Him, the light of His Son streams down, filling us with truth, and our lives sprout up in a beautiful display of His magnificent handiwork.

> LORD, THE SOIL OF MY HEART IS IN YOUR CAPABLE HANDS. YOU ARE THE VERY BEST GARDENER. GROW IN ME ALL THE TRAITS THAT MAKE ME MOST LIKE YOU.

Today, ask God to tend to the soil of your soul. Then watch in wonder at the beautiful growth God will bring to your life.

IN THE GARDEN

*For as the soil makes the sprout come up and a garden
causes seeds to grow, so the Sovereign LORD will make righteousness
and praise spring up before all nations.*

ISAIAH 61:11 NIV

Gardens have been cherished and celebrated since the beginning of time. From Genesis to Revelation, the Bible is full of nature's beauty, and for good reason! Many of us find peace in the natural world, feeling a connection to our Creator and coming away with a sense of renewal after spending time in His presence there.

The Lord obviously speaks to the heart through the beauty of His creation. But it's easy to forget that, at one time, all the wonders we behold had not appeared but were instead contained in the tiniest seeds! Those seeds were scattered (either naturally or by a human hand), watered, and warmed by the sun, finally finding their way to the surface to bloom and grow into what we see today. No one would ever guess what those little vessels of wonderment would become just by looking at them. So much is orchestrated inside them, unseen, transforming their simple beginning into something unexpectedly marvelous. Our lives are very much like those seeds, held in the hands of our Creator. Making all things new is His specialty (see Revelation 21:5). Like a master gardener, He knows exactly what wonders will be springing up from our days, even during those times when we doubt anything possibly turning out for our good. What we often see as ordinary, He sees as opportunity. What we see as an ending, He sees as a new start. He sees our amazing potential.

> LORD, THANK YOU FOR ALL THE WAYS YOU SHOW UP LIKE A GARDENER . . . PLANTING, NURTURING, AND EVEN PRUNING THOSE THINGS IN MY LIFE THAT YOU'RE BRINGING TO FRUITION. HELP ME TRUST THAT YOU ARE ALWAYS DOING GOOD WORK WITHIN ME.

THE PEACE IN PERFECT LOVE

When my heart is faint and overwhelmed,
lead me to the mighty, towering Rock of safety.

PSALM 61:2 TLB

Is anything too hard for God? Never. Would He leave us alone or without the strength we need to overcome anything we face today? Absolutely not. Will we let anything steal our peace, knowing God is for us? No way! Replacing anxious thoughts with confident declarations can keep us from feeling overwhelmed. Peace comes on the heels of thinking about what perfect love would say to us. If the thought isn't something God would say, it's got to go!

Perfect love is the power of truth put into practice. Perfect love kicks out every fear that comes to take the place of faith. Perfect love lifts every hope God sends to carry us through. Perfect love erases every lie that tries to tell us God has stepped out of our lives. No matter what kind of wilderness it feels like we're walking through, love is in it with an endless river of strength behind it. And there's more beauty than we can imagine up ahead.

God wants us to experience the peace He gives in the midst of the overwhelming days and the seasons of waiting. Love doesn't leave when it gets hard. It faithfully leads with our best always at the center of its purpose. We can be at peace when things around us look like they're falling apart because we know God is putting them together for our good. That's why we put our trust in perfect love. That's why, when our hearts are faint and overwhelmed, we choose to steer our thoughts in the direction of truth.

DEAR GOD, YOU ARE THE STRONG, SAFE PLACE IN WHICH MY HEART CAN TAKE REFUGE TODAY. FILL MY THOUGHTS WITH YOUR TRUTH AND LOVE AND GIVE ME RENEWED HOPE THAT EVERY DETAIL OF MY LIFE IS IN YOUR HANDS.

POWER TO SUSTAIN

Do you not know? Have you not heard?
The LORD is the everlasting God, the Creator of the ends of the earth.
He will not grow tired or weary, and His understanding
no one can fathom.

ISAIAH 40:28 NIV

A certain battery brand used to advertise that its batteries would keep going long past the average battery life. The brand was made famous by its pink bunny mascot, wearing sunglasses and playing a drum, tirelessly marching across the television screen. Viewers were meant to believe that this battery would go on practically forever. That is a quality that people tend to value: unending, unfaltering power. We flock to films about superhuman strength or ability. We take our warm homes, working ovens, and functioning cars for granted. Of course, we know that batteries eventually give up. Superheroes, as strong as they appear, have weaknesses that threaten their victories. Even electricity is not a sure thing, as we can see when the power goes out during a thunderstorm.

The only unending source of power and strength comes from God! He's the very best One to turn to if we need to keep going. His power has a built-in recharge. When we stay plugged in and connected to Him, His restoration of our hearts, habits, attitudes, and energy is automatic. When we are weak, He is strong. Interestingly, the more we acknowledge our inabilities before God, the more He can do in our lives. The more we lay down the idea of control and power on our own, the more powerful we allow God to be in our circumstances. God will sustain us. No matter what. He keeps going, and going, and going. . . .

LORD, THANK YOU FOR BEING MY SOURCE OF POWER AND STRENGTH. AT TIMES I FORGET AND TRY TO TAKE CONTROL. IN THOSE TIMES, REMIND ME THAT YOU ARE A MUCH MORE RELIABLE AND POWERFUL SOURCE.

PATIENCE IS A FRUIT

The LORD is good to those who depend on Him,
to those who search for Him.
So it is good to wait quietly for salvation from the LORD.

LAMENTATIONS 3:25–26 NLT

Farming is one of the toughest ways to make a living. There is so much that's out of the farmer's control, from the weather to the quality of seed, the ultimate health of the animals, the cost of products, and more. A farmer must learn, over time, to trust in the long game. He also must learn the valuable art of patience, because what he plants in one season will be the harvest of the next, and there is literally no speeding up of the process. Growth will happen in its own sweet time. Patience, for a farmer, is a necessary characteristic.

Time and again, the Bible promises us that patience is its own reward, but not its only reward. Yet we human beings are, by nature, an impatient lot. We know what we want, and we know when we want it: right now!

We live in an imperfect world inhabited by imperfect family members, imperfect friends, imperfect acquaintances, imperfect coworkers, and imperfect strangers. Sometimes we inherit troubles from these imperfect people, and sometimes we create troubles for ourselves. In either case, what's required is patience: patience for other people's shortcomings as well as our own.

Proverbs 16:32 teaches, "Better to be patient than powerful; better to have self-control than to conquer a city" (NLT). But for most of us, waiting patiently is hard. We are fallible beings who want things today, not tomorrow. Still, God instructs us to be patient, and that's what we must do. It's the peaceful way to live.

LORD, THANK YOU FOR PROVIDING THE GIFT OF PATIENCE THROUGH THE HOLY SPIRIT. DO WHAT YOU NEED IN ME IN ORDER TO CULTIVATE KINGDOM PATIENCE.

HOLDING OUT

The LORD God is our sun and our shield.
He gives us grace and glory.
The LORD will withhold no good thing
from those who do what is right.

PSALM 84:11 NLT

As he offered excuses, she stared at him, completely stunned by this turn of events. He was the perfect Christian guy, and she had given so much of her time and effort to the relationship. She had prayed for God's direction and felt so much peace pursuing this path. It just seemed perfect. Except now it wasn't because he was backing out. Anger invaded her thoughts, followed by bitterness—aimed first at her ex-boyfriend but later at God. She felt tricked, mistreated. *If God loved me, why would He let this happen?* she let her mind wonder.

We all have to watch our hearts and minds when life doesn't work out the way we planned. Our enemy is ready and eager to sow seeds of discontent and distrust as we question what God is doing. Like Eve in the Garden when the serpent second-guessed God's goodness, we're tempted to believe that God is holding out on us.

But God invites us to walk away from that temptation into a place of utter trust. When we can't figure out why God has blocked our path, we can lean even harder on His leading, let go of our demanding, and allow the Spirit to change our thinking while healing our wounded hearts. When we keep our hands open to God, we experience deeper rest. In the resting, we realize that God's plan—always drawing us closer to His presence—was far better than what we imagined in the first place.

FATHER, WE AREN'T BORN WITH GREAT PATIENCE, AND IT'S A HARD FRUIT TO CULTIVATE! HOLDING OUT FOR JUST THE RIGHT THING CAN BE HARD AND SCARY. BUT I KNOW THAT YOUR PLANS, CHOICES, AND WAYS ARE ALWAYS BEST. I WILL TRUST YOU AND WAIT.

A SHELTER IN THE TIME OF STORM

You are a tower of refuge to the poor, O LORD, a tower of refuge to the needy in distress. You are a refuge from the storm and a shelter from the heat. For the oppressive acts of ruthless people are like a storm beating against a wall, or like the relentless heat of the desert.

ISAIAH 25:4–5 NLT

Copper was the sweetest little dachshund on the planet, but he had one very troubling issue: he was a scaredy-cat. Er, scaredy-dog. Whenever a storm blew through, he would make a run for the bathroom and jump into the tub.

His owner, Annie, wasn't quite sure what to make of it. Many times, she would awaken in the night to the sound of barking coming from the bathroom. There she would find her precious pooch shivering and shaking in his porcelain hideaway. Turned out, he was great at getting in, but he couldn't get himself back out again.

Why the bathtub? A bit of research led her to the answer. Dogs feel grounded and safe in the tub during a storm. They leap over the edge to their porcelain safety net whenever they feel stressed or need an escape. Copper was doing what came naturally—protecting himself from the storm.

What about you? Where do you run when you need an escape from the storms of life? Is it a false sense of security, or is it solid protection? God wants to be your go-to hiding place. He longs for you to come to Him, not just when you're afraid, but whenever a storm of any kind hits. His name should be the first on your lips.

Are you walking through a storm right now? Call on the Lord. Jump into the safety of His arms. He will keep you grounded and safe, no matter how hard the winds might blow.

LORD, TODAY I CHOOSE TO RUN TO YOU WITH MY TROUBLES. NO MORE CALLING OUT TO OTHERS FIRST. YOU'LL BE MY GO-TO FROM NOW ON. THANK YOU FOR BEING MY SHELTER IN THE TIME OF STORM.

QUIET SPACE NEEDED

You're my place of quiet retreat;
I wait for Your Word to renew me.

PSALM 119:114 THE MESSAGE

Even before the worldwide pandemic, I was a social-distance proponent. I've always chosen the beach that I know is least populated, and if it does get crowded, I walk until I find an isolated spot. I know I'm not the only one who defines personal space as "enough area around me to avoid small talk or touching of any kind." We introverts just need more alone time than extroverts.

Even if we're not introverts, all of us need the place of quiet retreat that is our heavenly Father. We can read and remember every truth written, which is invaluable for our spiritual strength and well-being, but God renews us on a very personal level in the quiet times. It's a hard thing to explain, but it's a certainty, nonetheless.

"A hurricane wind ripped through the mountains and shattered the rocks before God, but God wasn't to be found in the wind; after the wind an earthquake, but God wasn't in the earthquake; and after the earthquake fire, but God wasn't in the fire; and after the fire a gentle and quiet whisper" (I Kings 19:11–12 THE MESSAGE).

God hasn't changed since Elijah heard that whisper. He wants us to get to a place away from the noise of the world so we can listen. Our part is to make the space in our lives to do it. When we're struggling the most, time to listen becomes most important. Our "place of quiet retreat" is also the God of the impossible, our Great Reward, our Shield, and the One who takes hold of our right hand and says, "Do not fear; I will help you" (Isaiah 41:13 NIV). Maybe today is a good day to make our getaway plan.

LORD GOD, I CAN'T ALWAYS ESCAPE TO SOLITUDE AND QUIET SPACES. BUT I KNOW I CAN FIND WINDOWS OF TIME TO SIT QUIETLY IN YOUR PRESENCE. HELP ME FIND THAT TIME TODAY.

TURN YOUR EYES UPON JESUS

Come with Me by yourselves to a quiet place and get some rest.

MARK 6:31 NIV

If you tend to be an overthinker, change may feel extra overwhelming to you. Overthinkers have an incredible ability to add many complicated layers to a situation by the stories we tell ourselves about it, the fears that spring up out of nowhere, and the whole host of anxious thoughts that run rampant on the hamster wheels of our minds.

Jesus was clearly aware of our common human condition when He walked among us, often addressing the worries of the people and redirecting their thoughts from fear to faith. And the beautiful and brilliant thing is anyone, anywhere, can do what He's inviting us to do: just turn our eyes toward Him.

We live in a time of information overload. We're constantly bombarded with solutions to problems we didn't even know we had. But the truth is, while information can be helpful, it will never do what a quiet moment in God's presence can do. When we are experiencing something new and unfamiliar, it can be easy to panic and grasp for whatever will bring a sense of safety and assurance. And while the world has plenty of solutions, the Father has one: Jesus. Our Light, our Shepherd, our Prince of Peace awaits our company every moment of the day. We can take a breath and shift our focus away from our overrun mind and toward a simple thought of Him. We can become aware of His presence and be reminded of His promised provision and unconditional love. To sum it up, we can just simply be.

LORD, IT'S EASY TO GET CAUGHT UP IN THE THINGS THAT DISTRACT ME FROM BEING WITH YOU. THANK YOU FOR YOUR DAILY INVITATION TO REST AT YOUR FEET WHENEVER I NEED IT.

WHAT THEY THINK

"If the world hates you,
keep in mind that it hated Me first."

JOHN 15:18 NIV

Jumping to conclusions can wear a person out! Yet that's all some folks do. We see people jumping to conclusions every day on television. We read it. We hear it on the radio. We see it on the internet. And sometimes conclusions jump out of our own mouths. The Bible categorizes this behavior as a path to folly: "He that answereth a matter before he heareth it, it is folly and shame unto him" (Proverbs 18:13 KJV). In the real world, the obvious thing to do is to go straight to the person and ask them to tell their side of the story. A dedicated news reporter would go even farther, interviewing other witnesses and gathering facts through research. In this crazy, convoluted world, we have to decide whether we want to be independent thinkers or go with the herd. The mob rules when people tickle our ears and tell us what they want us to know and when we allow our emotions to tell us what to think. And the mob wins when we value someone else's word more than we value the truth. The real truth is in God's Word (John 17:17).

The only exercise some people get is running their mouth, jumping to conclusions, and pushing their luck. Things are often not what they appear to be. Take the time and effort you would want others to put into searching for the truth about you, and do what is right even when no one else does.

LORD, THE ONLY WAY I AM ABLE TO ACT IN WAYS THAT REFLECT YOU IS IF I ABIDE IN YOU ALONE. HOLD ME CLOSE AND SPEAK CLEARLY TO MY HEART.

WORDS OF LIFE FOR THE ANXIOUS

Anxiety weighs down the heart,
but a kind word cheers it up.

PROVERBS 12:25 NIV

She couldn't put her finger on the source, really. She began to notice it creeping into every crevice of her life. At work, right before the big meetings; on the drive home, with all the crazy drivers; when she opened the mailbox and saw another bill. The anxiety meter kept inching higher and higher. She could feel it in her stomach . . . and her soul.

What should she do? What should all of us do? Anxiety seems to plague our society like never before. Despite the huge uptick in antianxiety medicine prescriptions, we still find ourselves frenzied and fretting about so many things. Yet Jesus says, "Fear not!" *But how can we keep from worrying?* we wonder. *Can't He see how huge our problems are?*

Jesus' words are powerful in a way ours aren't. His command comes with supernatural power and the promise of lasting peace. The key? Remembering His presence with us! The God who controls the storm stands with us, ready to steady our hearts even as we start to panic. What hope for us! One of the most important steps toward living a fear-free life is lowering our guard before God, pouring out our hearts, and letting Him minister to us. As we begin to live shamelessly before Him, we learn to leave fear in the dust.

And what a breath of fresh air we can bring to those around us when we help them remember our sovereign Savior, who quiets the storm with three simple words: "Peace, be still" (Mark 4:39 KJV).

> LORD GOD, YOUR HOPE IS MY ANCHOR, AND YOUR PEACE IS MY SAIL. AS I NAVIGATE ANXIOUS THOUGHTS AND FEELINGS, I WILL TRUST IN YOU.

EXPRESSIONS

*The LORD make His face shine on you and be gracious to you;
the LORD turn His face toward you and give you peace.*

NUMBERS 6:25–26 NIV

You're already nervous. Though you feel confident about your résumé and your ability to do the job, you just didn't have a good feeling about the first round of interviews. You sat up straight and tall, but the interviewer rarely looked up from the paper. When you attempted to answer questions, his arms remained crossed, face flat—stern even. The whole affair seemed so tense you were shocked when they called you back for a second interview. Then the CEO walked in with a strong stride and a serious expression. You sensed your doom approaching. But suddenly, a great big smile stretched across his face, and he reached out his hand in greeting. "I know you," he said with a grin, then explained that he had grown up in the same class as your dad. His tone was casual, his expressions positive, and you could feel the pressure ease. It was okay to be yourself, to communicate clearly and confidently without fear of future rejection.

For some people, approaching God in prayer is like an uncomfortable interview. They picture Him stark and angry, brows furrowed, presence demanding. No wonder they reserve prayer for emergency situations. But God is not that way. The cross of Christ nullified every ounce of His anger toward your sin. He knows us, His beloved children. We are not only forgiven but also cherished. God's expression toward us is full of light and love; the depths of who we are always meets with His smile.

LORD, THANK YOU FOR BEING APPROACHABLE AND KIND. GIVE ME A TRUE IMAGE OF WHO YOU ARE, SO THAT I CAN IMAGINE YOUR LOVE SMILING AT ME WHENEVER WE TALK.

When you talk to God this morning, imagine the best expression of joy you've ever seen. Then multiply the effect in your mind, and marvel that God's face shines on you today!

THERE IS PURPOSE IN REST

"Remember, your Father knows exactly what you need even before you ask Him!"

MATTHEW 6:8 TLB

There's something special about having a campfire with friends late in the fall, when the chill in the air hints at winter. Everyone knows spending time outside will soon give way to spending a lot more time inside. The fresh air feels exhilarating, the warmth of the fire invokes a little more gratefulness, and the conversations go a bit longer.

The cold months pull us into our homes, and we find ourselves falling into hibernating tendencies. Savoring the simple feels easier. A bowl of homemade soup tastes gourmet. Blankets feel softer. The fireplace is especially comforting. While we're cozied up in simple survivor mode, it can sometimes be easy to think we should be doing more. We can think our lives are passing by in the uneventful days of the ordinary and making no real impact.

God has purpose in rest. He showed the importance of it after creating all that we see. He put it in His top-ten ways to express our love for Him. He knew we needed time to simply be. So let's do it. Rest without regret. Rest without letting the rigorous schedule of life interrupt. Rest with every fiber of our being, knowing His love is around us, preparing us for what's ahead. We don't always have to be doing, going, moving, or planning to feel like we're living. Our life is in God alone. The simplicity of that truth is encouragement enough to face our days, however they unfold, with joy, confidence, and peace.

DEAR GOD, I'LL REST IN YOU AND YOUR PERFECT LOVE TODAY. NOTHING CAN SEPARATE ME FROM IT, NOTHING IS STRONGER, AND NOTHING CAN STAND AGAINST WHAT YOU HAVE PLANNED!

PEACE

"Peace I leave with you, My peace I give to you;
not as the world gives do I give to you.
Let not your heart be troubled, neither let it be afraid."

JOHN 14:27 NKJV

When Jesus returned to the disciples after His crucifixion, He stayed on earth for forty days before going to heaven for the last time. He could have offered any sort of wisdom. His final words could simply have been, "I told you so!" as He walked away. Or, He could have stayed away and not returned for those forty days at all. After all, He is God and can do what He wants! What He *did* do was to offer the gift of peace, to them and to us. Peace that transcends any sort of understanding.

Peace. It's such a beautiful word. It conveys images of serenity, contentment, and freedom from the trials and tribulations of everyday existence. Peace means freedom from conflict, freedom from inner turmoil, and freedom from worry. Peace is such a beautiful concept that advertisers and marketers attempt to sell it with images of relaxed vacationers lounging on the beach or happy senior citizens celebrating on the golf course. But contrary to the implied claims of modern media, real peace—genuine peace—isn't for sale. At any price.

Have you discovered the genuine peace that can be yours through Christ? Or are you still scurrying after the illusion of peace the world promises but cannot deliver? If you've turned things over to Jesus, you'll be blessed now and forever. So what are you waiting for? Let Him rule your heart and your thoughts, beginning now. When you do, you'll experience the peace that only He can give.

GOD, THANK YOU FOR OFFERING THE KIND OF PEACE THAT CAN'T BE WON OR BOUGHT IN ANY OTHER WAY. YOUR PEACE IS WORTH RECEIVING. HELP ME TO CARRY IT WELL.

CARRIED

The horse is made ready for the day of battle,
but victory rests with the LORD.

PROVERBS 21:31 NIV

When she awoke, she didn't need to check her calendar. She knew what day it was. For over a month she had been prepping her home and scouring every place to find empty moving boxes. Yesterday they were finally all filled with her family's belongings. Now she just needed the movers to arrive. Without their help, she'd be up a creek—without any of her stuff. She was a smart and strong woman, but she knew her limitations. When the load was too much for her, she let someone stronger take over and handle the rest.

It's a great strategy, the very kind our Savior says works in His kingdom, when we strike the right balance. Whenever God calls us to move from where we are, we may feel uncertain at first. How can we know God's will, and what's the best way to get there? Certainly, anxieties often lessen with a semblance of order, so putting a good plan in place may be the perfect solution for some of the stress!

But the secret to real rest lies in relying on who's strongest. While God has given us physical bodies to think and brainstorm, plan and plot, He alone has the understanding and strength we need for life to work. More than that, He infuses our earthly efforts with supernatural power, wielding impact beyond this life into eternity.

Today, don't wear yourself out, trying to wing it on your own. Let your Father do the heavy lifting as you lay your needs before Him in prayer.

LORD GOD, RELYING ON OTHERS SOMETIMES SEEMS SCARY AND MAKES ME FEEL VULNERABLE. BUT RELYING ON YOU IS ALWAYS BENEFICIAL. YOU ARE MY ROCK. THANK YOU!

WHY WORRY?

*"Therefore do not worry about tomorrow,
for tomorrow will worry about its own things.
Sufficient for the day is its own trouble."*

MATTHEW 6:34 NKJV

One good way to describe worry is that it's reacting to things that haven't happened yet. It's taking any *what-if* you can think of, giving it room to bloom, and putting yourself into the future story that the *what-if* could write. Worry dishonors God, as well as your own real story that is unfolding today as we speak. Worry spends so much time in the future that it prevents you from appreciating your *now*.

Because we are human beings who have the capacity to think and to anticipate future events, we worry. We worry about big things, little things, and just about everything in between. To make matters worse, we live in a world that breeds anxiety and fosters fear. So, it's not surprising that when we come face-to-face with tough times, we may fall prey to discouragement, doubt, or depression. But our Father in heaven has other plans.

God has promised that we can lead lives of abundance, not anxiety. In fact, His Word instructs us to "be anxious for nothing." But how can we put our fears to rest? By taking those fears to Him and leaving them there. The very same God who created the universe has promised to protect us both now and forever. He invites each of us to deposit our worries at His feet and let Him sort out our future. After all, He isn't bound by time. He is in our future right now, writing wonderful stories we haven't even dreamed of.

So, what do you have to worry about? With God on your side, the answer is nothing.

LORD, TODAY I SUBMIT MY WORRIES TO YOU. I REFUSE TO ALLOW ANXIETY OR FEAR TO STEAL MY PRECIOUS MOMENTS TODAY. FORGIVE ME FOR WORRYING OVER THINGS I CAN'T CONTROL.

STRENGTH IN SOLITUDE

My strength comes from GOD,
who made heaven, and earth, and mountains.

PSALM 121:2 THE MESSAGE

There's nothing too hard for God, and no one more important to Him than you. We won't face anything that He won't give us the courage to get through. But when worries and fears become loud in our minds, it's necessary for us to find a way to become quiet in our spirits.

Where we go to find quiet time is different for each of us, but it's hard to appreciate true quiet if we're not alone. We can enjoy time with our spouse or a good friend just being together in silence, but solitude is special. We connect with who we are and the One who made us in a deeper way, because they're intricately bound. We can't be secure in who we are without being one with our Creator. Solitude is imperative to staying grounded in our unique and powerful purpose.

God loves us, and He loves the life He's given us. His greatest joy is seeing us live the abundant life found in Him. In Him we have mountain-making strength and mountain-moving hope. And nothing gets to us without going through His love first. Good is going to come from everything we surrender to Him. We can't let the world or the worry keep us from seeking the solitude and the strength our souls need.

DEAR GOD, MY ALONE TIME WITH YOU IS MY STRENGTHENING SOLITUDE. GIVE ME THE COURAGE I NEED TO PUSH THROUGH EVERY WORRY AND KEEP ALL MY HOPE IN YOU.

Today is an invitation for us to respond to God's offer to strengthen us, fill us with peace, and fuel us with hope. If we can get alone for even a sliver of time to reconnect with the Source of every good thing, we can take another step forward. We can be confident that we're valued and our purpose is irreplaceable. God is ready to move any mountain in our lives to reveal His love.

WALK WITH GOD

God's kingdom . . . is about pleasing God,
about living in peace, and about true happiness.

ROMANS 14:17 CEV

What would make you happy? Many imagine that being free to take it easy, do their own thing, and go wherever their whims and interests lead them would be just the ticket. But ask anyone whose face reflects the soft smile of fulfillment and whose eyes glow with purpose and meaning. In other words, a happy person. You might get a different answer.

Probe their secret, and you're apt to hear about a life lived not for self, but for others, despite personal sacrifices. Dig deeper to learn about the strong faith that has seen them through difficulties and hardships, griefs and losses. You'll discover that happy, satisfied people are always engaged in pursuits higher than temporary pleasure and invested in quests beyond private gain. So much for doing your own thing!

Genuine happiness starts with deep and lasting values applied and practiced day by day. It develops as God's Spirit increases your faith and trust in His wisdom, even when times are tough or call for difficult choices. The result is in happiness unattainable by any other means—the happiness of walking together with God.

LORD GOD, I LONG FOR THE DEEP AND LASTING JOY THAT LIFE WITH YOU BRINGS. TODAY I OFFER YOU MY WHOLE HEART, AND I PROMISE TO SEEK YOU.

MAKING TIME TO SPEND TIME

Seek the Lord; yes, seek His strength and seek His face untiringly.

I CHRONICLES 16:11 TLB

Have you ever enjoyed people-watching at the beach? Everyone there seems to have this amazing positive energy. You can just see joy, peace, reflection, awe, inspiration, rest, relaxation, and smiles. There are so many smiles. Imagine how happy it must make God to see the beach bring all of those things to us—His crowning creation.

Earth's beauty is a constant reminder of God's love for us. Nature draws our hearts to Him because He designed all of this with us in mind. There's a direct connection to Him in all of it, and our spirits love the camaraderie. I love the definition of that word: "a mutual trust and friendship among those who spend a lot of time together." We need time away from the bustle of the world and our daily demands to nurture our trust and friendship with God. He's our life. He's every breath we take. He's our shelter, strength, hope, and peace. If we neglect to spend a lot of time with Him, the abundant life that Jesus came to give is lost in the rush. We have to be deliberate about disconnecting from the world to connect with our Father.

Ever wonder how exercising gives you more energy even though you are too tired to exercise in the first place? But if you discipline yourself to do it, it works. Expending energy to exercise gives you more energy. Likewise, we might think we just don't have time to spend time with God. But if we discipline ourselves to do it regularly, things start falling into place a lot more smoothly, and we feel less pressed—for time, patience, self-control, and all the other good things we're going to get in abundance from connecting with Him.

FATHER, GIVE ME WISDOM TO KNOW THE BEST WAYS TO SPEND TIME WITH YOU.

A TIME TO MOSEY

"Be still, and know that I am God;
I will be exalted among the nations,
I will be exalted in the earth."

PSALM 46:10 NIV

In our modern society, we are far better at whirling than moseying. We don't take enough time for pausing, resting, pondering, praying, or just being. We stay in a power mode: industrious, fidgeting, and ever harried. We can't seem to be still to enjoy a moment of true quiet without our cell phones and planners and gadgets. And in this endless busyness, we lose a valuable sense of who we are, what we were meant to be, and who God is. We lose sight of what is eternal and the Eternal One Himself. Filling our hours and days with nothing but busyness is a little like filling our stomachs with bowls of junk candy. Yes, it fills the space, but in the end, it isn't truly satisfying.

Our spirits cry out for more. Much more. God says to be still at times. And in that quiet, He would like us to know that He is God, and He alone is worthy of "the knowing." But what does it mean to "know"? The Hebrew word is *yada*, which can be defined as "something we discern by seeing." To see, we must look. And looking is a verb. While we are still before God, we are to be looking—actively—to see His God-ness. As we actively seek His presence and the truth of who He is, our stillness allows us to catch His very heart.

He is worthy of our time. There is much for the Lord to say in the silence of our souls. Are we listening?

LORD GOD, THANK YOU FOR INVITING ME INTO THE MOSEY OF LIFE WITH YOU. BUT LAYING DOWN MY FIDGETS, FUSSES, GADGETS, CALENDARS, AND WORRIES AT YOUR FEET IS HARD SOMETIMES. LEAD ME, AND I WILL FOLLOW.

BREATHE IN

This is what God the LORD says—the Creator of the heavens . . . who gives breath to its people, and life to those who walk on it.

ISAIAH 42:5 NIV

Take a deep breath in, the doctor instructs. You comply as she readjusts her stethoscope to hear different places around your lungs. "Now breathe out." You exhale, waiting to hear about any discoveries she may have made while the oxygen exchange was taking place. It's important to make sure the lungs are functioning properly. The quality and amount of oxygen you process with every breath in has a direct impact on the way the rest of your body functions.

When you stop to think about it, breathing itself is its own miracle––one that happens anywhere from seventeen thousand to thirty thousand times a day, depending on your age! In order to keep on living, laughing, talking, and loving, we have to keep on breathing. It's the way God designed for us to get the energy from the outside to the inside of us, fueling our bodies as needed. It's a second-by-second reminder of our critical reliance upon the divine breath of God, who brings us life in the first place. Should He want to, God could withdraw His breath from His creatures, and all life would instantly cease. Fortunately, He wants the opposite: to fill His people with His breath of life––not only to keep your physical heart pumping and your body running, but also to fill you with His Spirit so you can live this life to its fullest.

When you breathe in deeply by reading and believing His Word, you are filled with supernatural energy, joy, and power to exhale God's amazing grace into the world around you. Today, take a deep breath, drawing on God's incredible goodness and love for you. Then look for all the ways God brings you today to breathe out His grace everywhere you go.

> GOD, I LOVE RECEIVING A FRESH WORD FROM YOU, BECAUSE IT ALLOWS ME TO EXHALE TRUE PRAISE AND WORSHIP. I WILL SEEK YOU IN HOPE AND JOY TODAY.

BELIEVING BETTER

"It is not by force nor by strength,
but by My Spirit," says the LORD of Heaven's Armies.

ZECHARIAH 4:6 NLT

The longer she sat in her class, the more her stomach turned and twisted. *How am I ever going to get this done?* she worried as she scanned her calendar, calculating all the assignments she'd been given for the week. The mounting pressure surged like a rising tsunami. She felt certain she would drown.

How are humans supposed to survive so much stress? she silently wondered. By nature, we worry when pressures rise. It seems like our hearts can't help but buckle under the heavy loads we bear, and we labor hard to either tackle and tame every towering challenge or take a leave of absence from any effort at all.

But Jesus invites us to a better way—one that requires work, but lighter than the kind we've grown accustomed to do. He says, "Believe."

When we fear we're going to fail, we can believe that He's with us and will keep us from stumbling. When we question our future, we keep our eyes on Him because He's already there. And when we're tired from faith's fight, His name is our refuge. We find peace in God's unfailing promises—when we fully believe He's as good as His Word.

And what if we find ourselves failing in belief? By faith, move forward in obedience anyway. As we follow Christ's directions to come to Him for relief, we find our belief grows stronger—and our Savior was right, after all. His yoke is easy, and His burden is light. In our unbelief, we can ask for more faith. No matter what our feelings, our Father remains faithful.

LORD, YOU ARE WORTH BELIEVING, NO MATTER WHAT. I WILL CONTINUE TO ACT ON THE FAITH I HAVE, AND I ASK YOU FOR EVEN MORE FAITH TODAY.

BELLY UP

In all your ways submit to Him,
and He will make your paths straight.

PROVERBS 3:6 NIV

Goldie was a big girl—a full ninety pounds. As a pup, she always seemed to be in trouble. But what else was a purebred golden retriever to do? She was born to retrieve things, after all. She chewed up shoes, gnawed at the legs of her master's four-poster bed, and even mangled an expensive favorite purse.

Goldie's owner, Missy, was beside herself. If she couldn't get this ornery dog under control, she might have to consider rehoming her. And forget about correcting the naughty pooch! Every time she caught Goldie in the act, the sweet little thing just rolled over on her back and begged for a belly rub.

It took some time for Missy to realize that Goldie was offering her belly as an act of submission. But she did so as a ploy—to appease Missy in the moment.

We're a lot like that with God, aren't we? We deliberately disobey, then we're quick to act like we won't do it again. We offered rushed prayers: "God, I'm so sorry! I'll do better next time." But then we don't make an honest attempt to mend our ways when "next time" comes along.

It's time to go belly up, once and for all, girl! Submitting to the Lord means giving every area of your life to Him, not just today, but for the long haul. In all your ways submit to Him. That means even in your thought life. That cranky attitude? It has to go. Those gossip sessions with your bestie? Time to toss those to the curb. That snide comment you made to your hubby? Maybe you need to let that one go too.

Submission is the very best way to show the Lord that you mean business. What's holding you back? Today's the very best day to start.

LORD, I'M SORRY FOR THE MANY (MANY!) TIMES I'VE SAID, "I'LL CHANGE!" BUT THEN DIDN'T. TODAY I DO MY BEST TO SUBMIT TO YOU IN EVERY AREA OF MY LIFE. THANK YOU FOR YOUR PATIENCE, FATHER.

THE FORECAST FOR TODAY

"Come now, let us settle the matter," says the LORD.
"Though your sins are like scarlet, they shall be as white as snow."

ISAIAH 1:18 NIV

You heard the weather report, but you weren't sure it would pan out. It wouldn't be the first time you'd awakened in the morning hoping to find snow on the ground, only to see a soggy mess instead. But today was different. The light shining through the cracks in the blinds seemed brighter than before. So you tugged the shade's cord and pulled open the view to a brand-new world. All the dreary browns and grays of winter had vanished; in their place, pristine snow glistened against a brilliant blue sky. Nestled on tree branches, streets, cars, and everything in between, the weather miracle transformed the bleak world you'd known into a scene of magic, mystery, and undeniable beauty.

Better than any forecaster, God has issued a prediction for your day—no matter what the physical weather outside your doors. If you are trusting Him to make the landscape of your life brighter and better than before, you will wake up each day discovering a truth better than transient snow. God wipes your slate perfectly clean each new morning. The failures and regrets of yesterday are completely covered by His love and forgiveness. You are free to enjoy the beauty of all He is as you discover the treasures He has hidden for you in this day.

Unlike the weather, God's miracle of grace never changes, never fades away. You are forever forgiven, simply through faith in Him. Praise God for His mysterious, permanent, and undeniably beautiful gift of daily grace!

FATHER, I WILL TRUST YOU FOR A BEAUTIFUL DAY, NO MATTER HOW IT UNFOLDS. THANK YOU FOR YOUR AMAZING GRACE OVER MY LIFE.

THE FAITH BATTERY

Even if our gospel is veiled, it is veiled to those who are perishing,
whose minds the god of this age has blinded,
who do not believe, lest the light of the gospel of the glory of Christ,
who is the image of God, should shine on them.

II CORINTHIANS 4:3–4 NKJV

A pastor of a small church called all the young children to the pulpit one Sunday. Then he brought out a lantern and asked which of them knew what it was. Though all guessed correctly, he shook his head and explained that it was a solar lantern. He pointed at the solar cells on top and told them the lantern had a battery cell on the top portion, and during the day, when the sun was shining, the battery stored up the sun's energy. Then at night the lantern would shine in the darkness because of the energy it had saved up during the day. He explained that faith is a lot like a solar lantern. When our faith is strong and we pray and seek God, it's like we're storing up power in our faith battery. Then when we go through hard times, when things seem hopeless and dark, the light of our faith shines in the darkness around us and gives us comfort and hope.

How many of us sit shivering in fear and despair without hope or light to guide us through dark times in our lives? The Bible contains all the light we need to find our way in this world. In it are God's words of hope and life, testimonies of faith, and God's promises to us. Many people who turn its pages have turned their hearts and lives to Him.

LORD GOD, I KNOW YOUR WORD IS FULL OF LIFE. PRIORITIZING TIME WITH YOU IN THE WORD IS IMPORTANT, BUT SOMETIMES CHALLENGING. PLEASE MEET ME THERE AND TEACH ME!

PLUMB TIRED

Be devoted to one another in love.
Honor one another above yourselves.
Never be lacking in zeal,
but keep your spiritual fervor, serving the Lord.

ROMANS 12:10–11 NIV

Most of us are so busy all the time, our bodies exist in a state somewhere between tuckered out and running on empty. But being busy isn't always to blame. Did you know that living the couch-potato life while binge-watching your favorite shows can actually make a person feel more tired than someone who's active? Some people are so lazy they wouldn't bother to chase a snake away! Did you know that laziness and inactivity can be as deadly as smoking and obesity? Our bodies were made to move.

It doesn't take much. They say that walking for 30 minutes a day, getting in 10,000 steps, or getting vigorous exercise for 60 minutes a week can make profound differences in a person's health—physical as well as emotional. People who exercise regularly sleep better, and so do people who give up drinking too much coffee and energy drinks. The ancient Greek physician Hippocrates II, credited as the father of medicine, said, "If we could give every individual the right amount of nourishment and exercise, not too little and not too much, we would have found the safest way to health." As you examine your own lifestyle, what is one way you can show honor and value to your own body? Is it drinking more water, getting an appropriate amount of sleep, or going for walks? Is it turning off the television and opening the Word? Ask the Lord what a healthy *you* looks like to *Him*.

LORD, YOU HAVE DESIGNED ME PERFECTLY, TO BE ACTIVE AND STRONG IN PEACE-FILLED WAYS. LEAD ME TO HONOR WHAT YOU HAVE GIVEN ME AND BRING YOU JOY.

SIMPLY FOLLOW

Where you go I will go, and where you lodge I will lodge.
Your people shall be my people, and your God my God.

RUTH 1:16 ESV

After Naomi's husband and two sons died, she told her daughter-in-law Ruth of her plans to return to her homeland of Israel. After all, what was there for her in Moab? Ruth understood; she was a native of Moab, and the Moabites were enemies of the people of Israel. Yet, when Naomi urged Ruth to return home to her parents, Ruth declared that Naomi was her home. She followed Naomi to Israel and worked to gather barley so both she and Naomi could eat.

Ruth's devotion to her mother-in-law was evident to everyone. A relative of Naomi named Boaz said to Ruth, "I've been told all about what you have done for your mother-in-law since the death of your husband. . . . May the Lord repay you for what you have done. May you be richly rewarded by the Lord, the God of Israel, under whose wings you have come to take refuge" (Ruth 2:11–12 NIV).

What Boaz noticed about Ruth was her character. Character is developed gradually over time by a series of choices, actions, and attitudes. Ruth quickly developed a reputation in the town to be courageous, hardworking, loyal, and a woman of character. Boaz was so impressed by her integrity that he married her. Together, they became the great-grandparents of King David.

DEAR GOD, MAY I BE A WOMAN OF CHARACTER— TRUSTWORTHY, HONEST, AND LOYAL. MAY YOUR LOVE SHINE BRIGHTLY THROUGH MY LIFE.

How would you describe your character? Are you loyal and trustworthy? Are you honest and selfless? God loves to see us courageously displaying His character by radically showing love for others. It's a tall order, but He will grow His fruit in us (Galatians 5:22–23) so we can reveal Christ wherever we go.

THE PERFECT PLACE

Let the peace of Christ rule in your hearts,
since as members of one body you were called to peace.
And be thankful.

COLOSSIANS 3:15 NIV

It was late afternoon, and she had a little time on her hands before beginning dinner. Sitting down at her computer, she started to surf. Pop-up messages reminded her of people she hadn't seen in years, and before she knew it, she was scrolling through photo after perfect photo, looking at all the fun and fellowship everyone else seemed to be having. Even as she clicked "Like," she couldn't help wanting . . . wishing . . . wondering if her life (with all her worries) would ever be that good.

Then she went outside. The sun was setting behind the trees, brilliant streaks of pink and gold gilding a faint blue sky. A light breeze blew as the summer cicadas stirred in evening celebration. She sank onto her patio chair to enjoy the show, God's glory cast through chorus and color. In her pleasure, she felt God's presence. In His nearness, she gave thanks, her gratitude for all God's goodness washing away the discontent.

In giving thanks, we find our rightful place in this world and rest for our searching souls. We are the recipients of God's extraordinary grace, the object of His undeserved favor. In all the moments of our lives—the fun and the fearful, the successes and the failures—we live loved. All of eternity, beginning even before our birth, has been purchased for us at the highest price, our future secured by our loving Savior. The beauty of creation sings with worship and wonder at such extravagant love, lavished on us, God's beloved children. Let us join in with the song!

LORD, IN YOUR ARMS IS THE BEST PLACE TO REST. HELP ME TURN MY EYES AWAY FROM THE THINGS THAT DISTRACT AND DISCOURAGE, WHILE I LOOK TO YOU FOR MY VALUE AND STRENGTH.

A TIMELY TREAT

Therefore, my beloved brothers,
be steadfast, immovable, always abounding in the work of the Lord,
knowing that in the Lord your labor is not in vain.

I CORINTHIANS 15:58 ESV

Sylvia was blessed to work from home. She kept herself on a pretty regular schedule so that she would get the work done on time. Every morning she woke at about the same time, got prepared for her day, and settled into her chair to dive into her work. She took the usual lunch break and got back to work around one. Then, sometime around three in the afternoon, she would break for a snack and for a quick aerobic workout to stay awake.

Sylvia's cat, Jasper, seemed to have her routine memorized. He knew the minute his food would go into the bowl in the morning, and he counted on a treat at three. One afternoon Sylvia deviated from her routine. She got caught up in her work and couldn't break away. Jasper wound his way around her ankles, distracting and irritating her.

"Not right now, boy," she said as she nudged him away. "I'm busy." He disappeared, but she didn't give him much thought. Only when she found him sitting quietly next to the treat jar at four thirty did she realize he'd been patiently waiting for her all that time.

God wants us to be as consistent in our walk with Him as Jasper proved to be with his treats. He longs for us to meet Him every day—both in prayer and in His Word. He wants us to hover close and be ready for the blessings (think treats!) that He pours out. Most of all, He desires our love and companionship, day in and day out.

LORD, I'M DOING MY BEST TO BE CONSISTENT IN MY WALK WITH YOU. PLEASE SHOW ME AREAS THAT NEED TWEAKING. I'LL BE WAITING, LORD, NOT FOR A BLESSING, BUT FOR PRECIOUS TIME WITH YOU.

BE STILL TO HEAL

He says, "Be still, and know that I am God;
I will be exalted among the nations, I will be exalted in the earth."

PSALM 46:10 NIV

Jack finally had a chance to try out the new trampoline. He was excited to jump for the first time, but his mom wasn't so sure. Finally, his dad convinced her to let him try it out. Jack started to jump, higher and higher. He laughed along with his friends; they were all having a blast.

Jack was on the edge of the trampoline when he shouted, "Hey, guys, watch this!" He was attempting to jump and flip over the edge, but somehow he missed the landing and came down hard on his right arm. His arm snapped—the pain was unbearable. He called for his mom, who took him to the emergency room. The X-ray results confirmed a fractured right arm. The doctor explained to him that his arm would need to be in a cast for six weeks to keep it from moving. It had to be still in order to heal.

Have you been trying to heal without being still? Your injury could be physical or emotional; either way, the pain is very real. When you are hurting, it is natural to become still because moving hurts. This stillness is good because God does His best work when we are still before Him. Whenever you spend time in the presence of God, healing begins.

Are there any hurts you can give to God today? Ignoring or burying pain only allows it to fester and grow. You can trust the Lord with your pain. Bring Him your suffering and be still in His presence. Ask Him to heal your hurts and help you take steps toward wholeness. Allow Him to take full control, for He has all the answers.

LORD, I CONFESS THERE HAVE BEEN TIMES WHEN I HAVE BEEN HURT—EVEN TIMES WHEN I ACCIDENTALLY CAUSED MY OWN PAIN. IN THIS MOMENT, I AM ASKING YOU TO HEAL ME COMPLETELY. HELP ME TO MOVE FORWARD IN WHOLENESS—BODY, MIND, SOUL, AND SPIRIT.

HANDING IT ALL OVER

I've cultivated a quiet heart.

PSALM 131:2 THE MESSAGE

If we want plants to grow, we have to prepare the soil correctly and continue to give them our attention until they become healthy and vibrant. In the same way, it takes time, attention, and a little work to develop a quiet heart. We don't become patient in a day. We don't trust God completely after the first time He proves how faithful He is. And the trials of life, changing circumstances, and people we know all give us opportunities to practice that pretty often.

When it comes to maintaining a quiet heart, practice is good and failures are inevitable—but continued success will only come through an investment in prayer. We will never get to a quiet heart without going to God. Life will keep throwing curve balls, trials will keep coming, days will keep feeling impossibly difficult, and we'll need the strength He gives to make it through. The great thing is, the more times we have to run to Him, the more peace we get to enjoy. When we throw up our hands, He grabs them and pulls us up again. In exchange for surrender, He fills us with a calmness we can't get anywhere else.

Learning to trust is another part of cultivating a quiet heart. We like to think we don't need God to be involved in every little thing, so why bother Him with it all? But what would happen if we *did* bother Him with every single detail? It would draw us close to Him, and in turn, He will draw close to each of us. We want Him micromanaging our life. He's great with details—just study any single thing in nature and the way it's designed! Today will bring chances to cultivate a quiet heart—let's start by handing it all over to God.

FATHER, I INVITE YOU INTO EVERY MOMENT OF MY DAY AND ASK FOR YOUR GRACE IN THE THINGS THAT CHALLENGE MY QUIET HEART. THANK YOU FOR BEING CLOSE, LOVING ME BEST, AND CARING ABOUT EVERY LITTLE THING.

THE DIVINE DECREE

By the seventh day
God had finished His work,
and so He rested.

GENESIS 2:2 CEV

Every time you round that corner in your house, you see him curled up in a ball on his favorite chair—the one that once served people but now has become a rather royal bed for your beloved cat. "Must be nice," you mutter, as you give him a quick stroke behind the ears. "How do you sleep all day?" For just a quick second, you ponder what it's like to be a cat. How would it feel to rest like that and not feel bad about it?

It isn't just our pets that give us a picture of rest. Every other kind of living creature does too. Yet as humans, we feel exempt from this part of the created order. For sure, work is necessary—a God-ordained command and calling. But we have to wonder about our balance when we doze at traffic lights and yawn throughout our meetings. Our bodies are sending a signal that our kindhearted Creator wants us to hear: we all need rest, from the tips of our toes to the depths of our souls.

The great news is that we can choose rest without guilt. Better still, God says we must rest—not only physically but also spiritually—if we want to really know Him. His divine permission unfolds in the first few pages of Scripture when He rested from His important work, and His call to follow suit fills the rest of His written Word. Only when we stop striving can we recharge our bodies and refocus our minds to the truth of who we are: humans fully dependent on God and designed to follow His lead in every way.

FATHER, THANK YOU FOR DESIGNING US WITH A BUILT-IN NEED FOR REST. I WANT TO BECOME AN EXPERT IN THIS AREA! LEAD ME TO REST AT THE RIGHT TIMES AND IN THE RIGHT WAYS.

A TIME TO REST

And on the seventh day God ended His work
which He had done, and He rested.

GENESIS 2:2 NKJV

We sometimes hear this Bible verse referenced when people talk about feeling depleted. It's hard to deny the importance of setting aside time in our lives to reflect and recharge. It takes humility to admit that we can't do everything all the time! We were created with a need to pause, and as many of us have experienced, our physical and mental health will suffer if we ignore that need for too long.

So, how are you finding comfort in rest these days? Are you getting what you need? And what does "rest" look like to you? We each have our own answer to that question, and it's always changing, depending on the season of life in which we find ourselves. That's why it's so important for us to tune in regularly to ourselves and listen to what our minds and bodies are truly calling for when it comes to downshifting.

It may be as simple as committing to eight hours of sleep for a while (which can be a challenge for those of us who often burn the candle at both ends). It could be giving ourselves a screen limit to reduce the amount of noise that's coming in every day and maybe reaching for a book instead—one we know will feed our spirit. It may be setting aside some time to sit outdoors in our favorite beautiful spot or designating a family day that's all about relaxing together without an agenda. It may be many different things over the years, depending on circumstances and life stages, but one thing it can always be is a priority in our lives. Rest is one of those gifts we give ourselves that will benefit us for a lifetime.

> FATHER, I COMMIT TO RESTING IN THE DAYS AHEAD. SHOW ME WINDOWS OF TIME IN WHICH REST CAN BE THE PRIORITY.

HIDE AND SEEK

He who comes to God must believe that He is,
and that He is a rewarder of those who diligently seek Him.

HEBREWS 11:6 NKJV

The stadium is packed, and cheers from the crowd are roaring. The game has already started, and you know your friend who invited you is somewhere in that sea of faces waiting for you to join him. But the scene seems quite daunting. How will you ever find the one you are looking for in the midst of all those people? Determined, you start scanning, row by row, the faces in the crowd. Up and across, up and across—you search until your eyes lock. This whole time, your friend has been watching you, waiting for you to notice the waves and smile beaming your way that say, *Come up here and join me!*

When you walk out your door this morning, it might seem like just an ordinary day full of responsibilities to fill. But you have one Friend who has invited you to experience it and enjoy it with Him. God is hidden in the details of your day, watching you and waiting to reward you with the pleasure of His presence.

Will He be in the quiet moments you spend studying His Word? In the tender touch of your child's hand? In the conversations you have at school or work? In the car ride to get there? In your thoughts as you consider how to handle this day? The answer is yes! God is hidden in every moment of your life. He is waiting for you to notice Him, to acknowledge Him, to take your place beside Him and enjoy the view. Seek His face today and enjoy the reward of His presence with you everywhere you go.

LORD GOD, I LONG TO SPEND THE DAY BY YOUR SIDE. THANK YOU FOR SAVING ME A SEAT.

THE FRIENDSHIP OF THE LORD

The secret of the LORD is with those who fear Him,
and He will show them His covenant.

PSALM 25:14 NKJV

To whom do you tell your secrets? If you're smart, you will spill the details of your life with good close friends, people with a proven track record of trustworthiness. If not, you'll be sorry. God is like that too. When you walk with Him, He walks right alongside you and communicates His feelings, teaches you, and even shares His secrets with you. Abraham was an attentive host to three angels who visited him at his camp. As they were leaving, however, he noticed they were headed toward Sodom, the city where his nephew Lot lived, and that worried him. So, God asked Himself a rhetorical question: "Shall I hide from Abraham what I am about to do?" (Genesis 18:17 NIV). God had planned on telling Abraham from the get-go that He was about to blot out Sodom and Gomorrah; otherwise He wouldn't have sent the three angels to Abraham's tent. God wants to speak to us in confidential counsel and communion, and He does so mostly through His Word, the Bible, to share the Gospel with others, to warn and prepare us for future events, and to bring us to repentance.

The entire book of Revelation is all about God sharing a big secret with us about what will happen in the end times: "Behold! I tell you a mystery. We shall not all sleep, but we shall all be changed" (I Corinthians 15:51 ESV). He tells us precisely what to look for as we approach the events that are to come, and He gives us signs to help us navigate. To understand. To prepare.

LORD, I LONG FOR A CLOSE RELATIONSHIP WITH YOU. THE KIND IN WHICH I KNOW THE SOUND OF YOUR VOICE ANYTIME YOU SPEAK. THANK YOU FOR BEING MY FRIEND!

THE FINE COMPANY
OF JESUS

As they were talking about these things,
Jesus himself stood among them, and said to them, "Peace to you!"

LUKE 24:36 ESV

One of the best ways to quiet your heart before God is to get out in nature. Sit still in a local bird sanctuary, on a shoreline, along a trail, or somewhere overlooking the sunrise or sunset, and soon enough, your soul will connect with creation. It may even be simply staring out the window of your office during a mind block, admiring the sky or the trees you see. You will find, in the stillness, an opportunity to meet with Jesus and evaluate the state of your own spirit.

So, how *is* your spirit doing today? Do you feel like a gentle, ambling creek, or are you a windmill let loose in a tornado, rattling wildly and out of control? When Jesus came to earth, He arrived with so many good things for us. Love and mercy. Forgiveness and salvation. Reconciliation with God and eternal life. Everything our souls craved but couldn't find on our own. Yes, the Lord brought a hundred reasons to throw our heads back in pure laughter and joy. And if that wasn't enough, Christ came to offer us peace.

If the world has gotten you riled up with fear and rage and your spirit feels like a windmill in a hurricane, reach out your hand and heart to Christ. Ask Him to give you the peace that passes all understanding. The peace that endures. The peace that transforms. Wherever you go, whatever you're doing, come springtime or harvest, never forget to squint up at the sunburst, grin a bit, and enjoy the peace that can only come from the fine company of Jesus!

FATHER, I RELISH THE OPPORTUNITIES I RECEIVE TO ENJOY AND APPRECIATE NATURE. I LOVE MEETING WITH YOU AMONG YOUR OWN CREATION. EXAMINE MY HEART, LORD. I RECEIVE YOUR PEACE.

AN ORDINARY WAY TO SEE OUR EXTRAORDINARY VALUE

Break open Your words, let the light shine out,
let ordinary people see the meaning.

PSALM 119:130 THE MESSAGE

We tend to complicate things. We overthink, over-worry, and overtake—until we're overwhelmed. If we're not careful, we convince ourselves that being in control is comforting. In truth, it only brings a false and temporary sense of security. God's Word sheds light on a different way of living: "Look at the birds of the air; they do not sow or reap or store away in barns, and yet your heavenly Father feeds them. Are you not much more valuable than they?" (Matthew 6:26 NIV).

There's not a created being on earth more valuable to the heavenly Father than you. Every moment we spend striving to get a desired outcome, every ounce of energy we exert trying to make our lives look perfectly in place, and every day we let slip away without putting our absolute trust in God is time we spend forgetting the simple words of our faithful Father.

Everything we have in front of us today—the people we love, the job, the circumstance, the chance meeting, the unexpected interruption—is seen by the One who promises to provide every single thing we need to get through it. We never have to wonder how we're going to handle what God allows. Our value to Him puts our life in the center of His love and at the center of His attention. And His loving response is to be a Father who never forgets the extraordinary price He paid for His most valuable creation: you!

DEAR FATHER, YOUR FAITHFULNESS IS MY SECURITY IN AN UNSURE WORLD FILLED WITH UNEXPECTED CHALLENGES. I SURRENDER MY DAY TO YOU AND YOUR LOVING, ALWAYS-SUFFICIENT GRACE.

THE PATH TO PEACE AND QUIET

Pray for all people. Ask God to help them . . .
so that we can live peaceful and quiet lives
marked by godliness and dignity.

1 TIMOTHY 2:1–2 NLT

Some days it can feel like we're moving farther away from living peaceful, quiet lives with one another and closer to living in a world where too many are defensive and unforgiving. It's heartbreaking. It can leave us tired, weary, and wanting to curl up under a blanket until kindness and compassion come out again. But while we have the covers over our heads, we also have the incredible power to bring the change for which we long. We can pray for each other.

As simple as it sounds, too much of the time, we speed through our days without uttering a single prayer for our leaders, our friends, and those who need to see the love of God and the kindness of His heart. Being part of the solution means loving people bravely every day, no matter how deep our differences run. We have the chance to be light bearers in the darkness, love bringers in the heaviness, and prayer warriors in a battle-weary world.

Love in motion creates miracles all around us. Hearts are healed, encouraged, and changed. Hope is ignited. We begin to see a better world and a way to get there. There's a lot to do, but prayer, light, and love are the collective force that can do what it takes.

How can we start in a small, simple way to initiate a love chain reaction today? God has the plan if we have the persistence! The opportunities will land in front of us, inside or outside our homes, and we should take every one of them. When we do, we should pray for even more chances to love people and bring light into the world. It's the most beautiful way to bring the brightest change.

DEAR GOD, LET ME BE A LIGHT IN THE WORLD THAT OVERCOMES DARKNESS THROUGH PRAYER, LOVE, AND HOPE.

STORM SHELTER

*Whoever dwells in the shelter of the Most High
will rest in the shadow of the Almighty.*

PSALM 91:1 NIV

You can remember the moments like they were just yesterday—those chilling childhood memories when the terror of a night's dream or a clapping crash of a thunderstorm outside your window woke you up, and you started to worry. Crouching low under the covers simply wouldn't cut it. Fear moved you out of your bedroom in search of a safer, more substantial place of shelter. Slipping silently between your parents even as they slept, your pounding heart quieted. Your panic stilled as your breathing fell in sync with theirs. Nestled next to them, you felt safe, surrounded by such powerful love.

As you grew up, though, so did your knowledge of the world. You learned: earthly parents—and people in general—aren't fail-proof. Real-life problems don't always disappear with the dawn. Fearful unknowns like insufficient finances, broken relationships, and failing health can leave you feeling like you did as a child, powerless to calm the mounting pressures all around you. Only this time, our problems are greater than any parent can solve . . . except for our heavenly Father.

Child of God, you don't need to stay stuck in your fears, afraid of what is to come, wondering who can help. Leave the isolation of self-reliance and turn to God Almighty. He is a shield and source of comfort like no other. Not only is He right beside us, He is above us, below us, before us, and behind us! Better still, He put His Spirit in us so we can sleep, wake, and walk in total confidence as we remain always in His competent and constant care.

LORD GOD, I KNOW YOU ARE MY SHELTER AND MY PLACE OF REST. I GIVE YOU MY FEARS TODAY AND COMMIT TO DWELLING UNDER YOUR WINGS.

LEARNING FROM THE TEXTBOOK ON LOVE

Let Me teach you; for I am gentle and humble,
and you shall find rest for your souls.

MATTHEW 11:28 TLB

If you've ever been to a beach in a subtropical region in the middle of July, you know you need to take some things you might not "normally" take. I go alone, so I've never been in the habit of bringing a canopy or umbrella with me. I quickly discovered on that blistering July day that I was going to need a break from the heat. To my dismay it was a cloudless day. It ended up being the shortest beach day I've ever had. And I gained a new appreciation for clouds and canopies.

It's good to be a lifelong learner. There are things all along the way that teach us how to be better friends, parents, siblings, coworkers, and most importantly, people who love God and the people He made. And that includes everybody. Jesus is the best Teacher of the things that matter most. Through His life on earth, He left us a clear example of how to live. Still, we need to let Him teach us. We need to keep studying the words He spoke and the life He lived. It's our path to finding rest. Real rest for our souls. He's gentle and humble, so He won't force the lessons on us or make us accept the guidance He offers.

Like clouds on a sunny day give us a cool break and a little relief, learning how Jesus handled life gives us a break from the burden of trying to figure it out on our own. His life is the textbook on love, and love is what we're here to do. It's a simple command, but we won't master it in a lifetime. All we can do is learn how to get better at it, but only by letting our Master teach us.

FATHER, TEACH ME TO LISTEN AND FOLLOW, TO LOVE AND REST, TO DAILY SURRENDER TO A LIFETIME OF LEARNING YOUR WAYS.

CHOOSING TO REST

*"Come to Me, all you who are weary and burdened,
and I will give you rest."*

MATTHEW 11:28 NIV

A funny thing has happened to our ability to slow down. If we don't get extremely intentional about it, then most of the time, our mindful living and peaceful outlook simply don't happen. Surprisingly, it often takes a strong will and an even stronger willingness to say "no." There is always work to do. We tend to forget that in the kingdom of God, there is a perfectly appointed time for rest, as well. The Bible repeatedly invites us to quiet our hearts and minds before God, reminding our hearts of who is really in control and of what we actually have the ability to affect in our daily lives. Rest isn't just a "would like to do." It's an act of obedience.

In this demanding and distracting world, rest is so important. But many people aren't sure how to rest in a way that fills and refreshes them. Resting in Jesus isn't too unlike resting on a beach, in a hammock, with a cool glass of water and a good book in hand. Your mind releases its worries—to Jesus. Your body relaxes, as if wrapped in strong arms. Your thoughts turn to all the good qualities of the One who loves you more than anything. Resting in Jesus can happen at the office or at home, in nature or on a busy street. Try taking five minutes today and deliberately practice the art of resting in Jesus. When you do, you will not only feel refreshed. You will be walking in obedience to God's heart for you.

FATHER, YOU KNOW HOW HARD IT IS FOR HUMANS TO REST. WE THINK THAT WORKING HARDER, NOT SMARTER, IS THE WAY TO YOUR HEART. BUT BOY, DO WE HAVE IT WRONG. MY DESIRE IS TO HONOR YOU BY RESTING AT THE RIGHT TIMES AND IN THE RIGHT WAYS. PLEASE HELP ME TO DO THAT.

PRAY-TECTION

*This is the confidence we have in approaching God:
that if we ask anything according to His will, He hears us.*

I JOHN 5:14 NIV

If someone walks in on you when you're talking to God, they're going to think you're as crazy as a soup sandwich. But that's okay. Prayer is the wonderful way believers communicate with God. We confess our sins, tell Him our secrets, air life's hurts and frustrations to Him, and present our requests to Him when we pray. We praise Him. We sing. We dance. And other times it's nice to just sit in the big silence that God makes when He's there with you in the room. God doesn't need our prayers to act on our behalf; He requires them. Scripture calls for us to "pray for those who persecute [us]" (Matthew 5:44 NIV), to "pray in the Spirit on all occasions with all kinds of prayers and requests" (Ephesians 6:18 NIV), to "devote [ourselves] to prayer and being watchful and thankful" (Colossians 4:2 NIV), and to "pray continually" (I Thessalonians 5:17 NIV). Jesus was always going off by Himself to find a solitary place to pray. We should follow His example. Prayer is our greatest weapon against the enemy.

When we pray for ourselves and our family, friends, coworkers, neighbors, country, and the world, a calm confidence replaces the worry and anxiety in our hearts. The fear that grips us is replaced by faith when we pray. Jesus saves, heals, protects, and delivers! Prayer brings God's pray-tection. Prayer brings God's provision. Prayer brings God's peace.

FATHER, THANK YOU FOR THE PEACE THAT COMES WITH SURRENDERING ALL TO YOU. THANK YOU FOR HEARING MY PRAYERS AND ANSWERING THEM IN THE PERFECT WAY, AT THE PERFECT TIME. I TRUST YOU.

PURPOSEFULLY PEACEFUL

Lord, through all the generations You have been our home!
Before the mountains were created, before the earth was formed,
You are God without beginning or end.

PSALM 90:1–2 TLB

There's peace in being home. In the morning, it's where we open our eyes, take a deep breath, and gather courage for the day. In the evening, it's where we get comfortable, exhale, rest, and restore.

Home is the place we look forward to going at the end of the day. It's where our favorite people are, where we keep the things that are beautiful to us, and where we're safe being who we are, without hesitation. When our hearts are home to God, we invite Him to be all He wants to be in our lives, without reservation. He's there to be everything we need because that's who He is.

Our souls enjoy real peace when we give God a real place in our lives. We can't go through the motions every day hoping we don't run out of spiritual energy. Eventually, we will. It doesn't take a large quantity of time spent with Him, but it does take some quality time. A "thank You" at the sight of a sunrise or with our first sip of coffee is a simple acknowledgment of God's goodness. It starts the day in a way that gets our attitude going in the right direction. Relationships are strengthened through the little things. Gestures of love and appreciation build a strong foundation, and God enjoys them just like we do!

Today can be purposefully peaceful. We can set the tone right now. If we can imagine God wrapping His arms around us this moment, we can face every moment in our day peacefully, knowing He's here to be everything we need.

DEAR GOD, THERE'S NOTHING THAT WILL COME MY WAY TODAY THAT WE CAN'T HANDLE TOGETHER. GIVE ME PEACE FOR WHAT'S COMING AND SPIRITUAL STRENGTH TO CARRY ME THROUGH.

DEEP SLEEP

In peace I will lie down and sleep,
for You alone, LORD, make me dwell in safety.

PSALM 4:8 NIV

Have you ever watched a dog drift off to sleep? He s-t-r-e-t-c-h-e-s, then settles down at his master's feet, finding a comfortable position. Within seconds he dozes off without a care in the world. Nothing matters, as long as he and his master are close together. That pup can sleep in perfect peace, never stirring.

The same is true when we put our heads on our pillow at night. We have nothing to fear. All concerns can be pushed aside. Our Master is right there, just a breath away. He's tucked us in, easing all worries, and He longs for us to get the rest we need. (And getting a great night's sleep is critical for good health, after all.)

What about you? How are your sleep habits? Do you have a hard time drifting off? Are the cares and concerns of life weighing you down? If so, then picture yourself handing them to the Lord before you even climb into bed at night. He can handle them, after all. And He doesn't even need your help to do so.

Think about that for a moment. For eight solid hours, you're not in control . . . of anything. You hand over the reins to the One who created you, who cares more about you than you do yourself. During those hours, you don't fret over what's going on at work or that hurtful thing a friend said to you. You're at the complete mercy of your Master.

That's how a pup feels too. He's completely at ease, knowing his owner will keep him safe. What a lovely, precious image.

FATHER, I LOVE MY SLEEP TIME! THAT MOMENT WHEN I DOZE OFF IS SO HOLY, FOR IT'S WHEN I HAND OVER THE REINS COMPLETELY TO YOU. THANK YOU FOR WATCHING OVER ME WHEN I'M NOT AWAKE TO WATCH OVER MYSELF.

ANCHORS AWAY

Stay grounded and steady in that bond of trust,
constantly tuned in to the Message,
careful not to be distracted or diverted.

COLOSSIANS 1:22 THE MESSAGE

The skies were the deepest blue, but the crystal-clear ocean waters gleamed aquamarine in the warm sunlight. Sitting atop your small boat, you can clearly see the brilliant colors in the coral reef below, the promise of exotic fish and maybe a sea turtle or two tempting you to dive beneath the surface. Slipping into the cool water, you secure your mask and snorkel, ensuring a tight fit. As you float on the surface, gazing at the beautiful water wonderland, you suddenly think: *Did I drop anchor?* In a slight panic, you look upward in search of your boat. Finally you see it far in the distance. Switching gears, you swim freestyle and full throttle to the one place you never meant to veer far from.

Experienced snorkelers and scuba divers know the importance of dropping anchor and always staying within sight of the boat. And God's children would do well to apply the same principle in the spiritual realm. The world around us often shines brightly with beautiful attractions. Many of them are given for us to explore, but when we let them lure us away from the foundational truth of God and His Word, we discover danger in what once seemed benign or even beautiful. God repeats the theme throughout His Word: we are to keep our relationship with Him anchored in His Word. Only then can we safely navigate the life-waters of this world.

What about you? Are you anchored securely in God, your relationship rightly tied to His saving grace? Or have you drifted away from the center? Without delay, ask God to direct you toward His love and truth right now.

LORD, I WANT TO BE CENTERED IN YOUR WILL AND SQUARELY IN YOUR HEART. SEARCH ME AND LEAD ME IN THE WAY THAT ONLY YOU CAN.

ENDURING TRIALS

We are hard pressed on every side, but not crushed;
perplexed, but not in despair; persecuted, but not abandoned;
struck down, but not destroyed.

II CORINTHIANS 4:8–9 NIV

Every time the coach whistled to send in another substitute instead of her son, the mom felt her frustration growing into a volcano that was certain to blow any second.

Why doesn't the coach see his potential? Why is he wasting all our time?! Doesn't he know how humiliating it is for him to stay seated on the bench? She was seething. It was all she could do to stay seated instead of marching out onto the field to give that coach a piece of her mind.

But then God gave her the peace of His own mind and heart. *Is there any better way for your son to learn patience, trust, and humility than on that lonely, lowly bench?* God asked her spirit.

And she realized the truth. Trials bring us to a fork in the road: Will we protest the path and part ways with God, or will we simply trust Him? Will we seek to establish control of our own, or will we yield to His plan? When we ourselves encounter difficulty or when we see our loved ones suffering, it's tempting to focus on the circumstances and to fight our way out of them. But this is the moment when we most need to pray, asking God for His wisdom and perspective. In these moments, we can use our words to urge others down the right path or the wrong one. In the midst of the trials, let's focus on Jesus, the Author and Perfecter of our faith.

GOD, YOU PROMISE THAT WE WILL FACE TROUBLE. BUT YOU ALSO PROMISE THAT OUR ENDURANCE WILL PRODUCE CHARACTER AND FAITH. HELP ME TO SEE EVERY TRIAL, TEST, AND SITUATION AS AN OPPORTUNITY TO GROW.

TUCKED AWAY

They marched for three days after leaving the mountain of the LORD,
with the Ark of the LORD's Covenant moving ahead of them
to show them where to stop and rest. As they moved on each day,
the cloud of the LORD hovered over them.

NUMBERS 10:33–34 NLT

The room smelled of finger paint and playdough, the class of kindergarteners working steadily at their stations, when their teacher made the call: "Time to put up your work and get out your mats," she announced cheerfully. A few kids grumbled, resisting her assistance, but most went without incident to the mats designated for their daily rest. With lights off and mouths closed, the once-rowdy children soon drifted off to sleep, their tiny bodies refueling energy for all that lay ahead.

Like the teacher, people who know children understand the importance of rest for growing, healthy young minds and bodies. In a similar way, God knows what His children need—even when we're convinced we need to keep going. He goes before us, providing pockets of time for needed rest tucked into each day when we can turn our minds and cares over to Him. But unlike the teacher, He doesn't force the issue. We must be willing to be still when the moment presents itself. Instead of turning on the radio, surfing the Web, or scrolling through social media whenever there's a lull, let your attention turn to God and His Word. Allow yourself time to rest in stillness, simply thinking about who He is and how He cares for you. At the end of the day, you will find that your time was never wasted. Instead, your mind and soul's rest today will ready you for all God has in store for you tomorrow.

FATHER, YOU MAY NEED TO REMIND ME TO TAKE THE REST I NEED PHYSICALLY, MENTALLY, AND SPIRITUALLY. TODAY I ASK YOU TO BE A PART OF MY RESTORATION PROCESS EACH DAY.

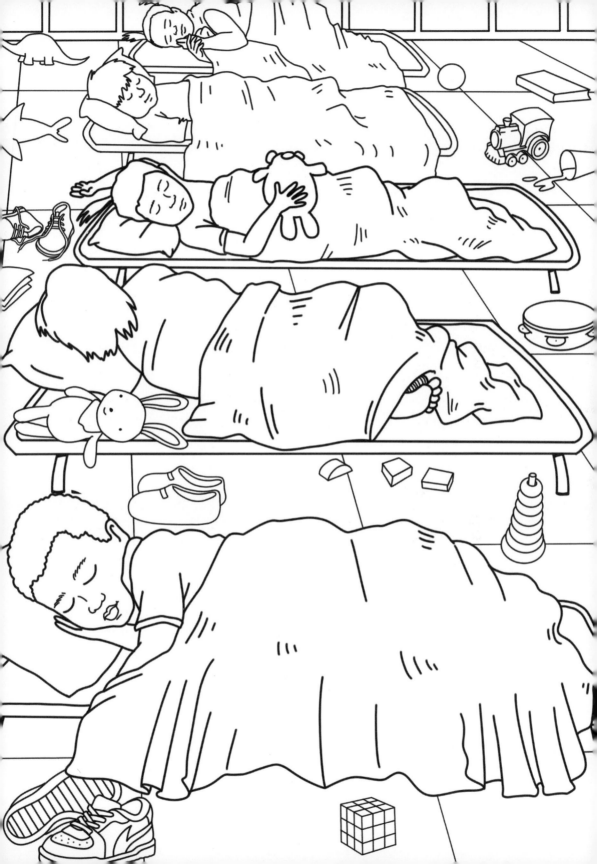

A QUIET LIFE

*"In repentance and rest is your salvation,
in quietness and trust is your strength."*

ISAIAH 30:15 NIV

On our beach walks, my dad and I would often pass a mansion that had been built by a businessman for his wife. Sadly, they were rarely there. It seemed strange to me. Such a grand gesture left empty and underappreciated. The structure was magnificent, but the heart of it was lifeless. Dad and I thought the same thing—it looks great on the outside, but there's nothing on the inside, the way our lives should never be.

My dad was a quiet man. He built a lot of houses in his lifetime, but the greatest thing he built was an unshakeable trust in God. We learned by his example that faith was the foundation of a good life and Jesus was the cornerstone of an eternal one. I'm thankful for the gift of his life. We don't know all the ways our lives will influence the people around us, but my dad is proof that we don't have to be loud about it. Living a quiet life is encouraged over and over in Scripture, and I believe it's because faith and love are more about what we do than what we say.

If our hearts are secure in our salvation and trusting God completely, the life inside us will manifest outwardly in acts of kindness, generosity, and selflessness. At my dad's wake, we found out there were some things he had graciously done for people that we'd had no idea about. I saw him buy groceries for families, sacrifice his time, take the coat off his back and give it away, and countless other small reflections of Jesus, but he had quietly done so much more. I hope we find ways to love quietly today, because that's the best way to speak volumes about the God we serve.

FATHER, LET ME BE A VESSEL OF YOUR LOVE TO THE PEOPLE IN MY LIFE AND THOSE WHOM YOU BRING INTO IT.

CATNAPS

"Come to me, all who labor and are heavy laden,
and I will give you rest. Take my yoke upon you, and learn from me,
for I am gentle and lowly in heart, and you will find rest for
your souls. For my yoke is easy, and my burden is light."

MATTHEW 11:28–30 ESV

Callie envied her cat who had nothing more to do with her life than to lounge around and sun herself, day after day. Oh, Genevieve would occasionally rouse herself from her slumber to nibble on some kibble, but then she would go right back to her spot on the back of the sofa, where beams of sunlight streamed through the window and lulled her into yet another nap.

"Wish I could take a little snooze," Callie would say as she happened by with a basket of laundry on her way to the washing machine.

"Must be nice," she would add as she buzzed by with an armload of kids' toys, headed to the toy box.

Maybe you can relate to Callie. There's never a moment to catch your breath because your workload is too high. You wish you could lounge around, but it doesn't seem possible.

Today, God is asking you to reconsider your schedule. He's got big things for you to do, sure. But you're going to need supernatural energy that only comes from one source—time spent in His presence.

If you'll set your gaze on your heavenly Father, He will draw you into that holy place with Him. There, you can hand over the things that have worn you down. He will show you how to bring all areas of your life into balance, so that rest—true rest—is possible.

LORD, I FEEL LIKE I'M ALWAYS ON THE GO. BUT I SECRETLY ENVY THOSE WHO MOVE AT A SLOWER PACE. I WONDER HOW THEY MANAGE. SHOW ME HOW TO BRING THINGS INTO BALANCE. I LONG TO SPEND TIME WITH YOU AND RECEIVE THE KIND OF PEACE AND REST THAT ONLY YOU CAN OFFER. HELP ME, I PRAY.

PRESENT IN HIS PRESENCE

I'm in the very presence of God—oh, how refreshing it is!

PSALM 73:27 THE MESSAGE

Some of the traits of a person referred to as a "beach bum" are being chill, laid back, calm, and carefree. That sounds a lot like God wants us to be! While we can't stay in that mode all the time, we can reset our spirit to a place of quietness, stillness, and rest by spending time with Him. He's everywhere and always present, but knowing God is with us is not the same as spending time with Him—just like thinking about the beach is not the same as being at the beach. We must silence distractions, get alone, and welcome Him into our innermost thoughts.

There are many different "meeting" places. Music. Nature. Long walks. Oceanside. Silent prayers before opening your eyes in the morning or when you close them at night. Being present to spend time in God's presence doesn't have to be rigid and scheduled. Impromptu moments can become the most refreshing parts of our day because being still and being spiritually quiet can happen anywhere at any time. Are we taking every opportunity, no matter how brief, to be refreshed? God loves to be the reason our hearts and minds take a respite from the chaos of this world.

We can create habits that become spiritual havens. We often give more energy to our physical well-being, but that isn't the most vital use of our resources. "Physical training is of some value, but godliness has value for all things, holding promise for both the present life and the life to come" (I Timothy 4:8 NIV). Spending time with God renews our soul-strength and sharpens our reflection of Him. We'll start to embody love, patience, kindness, compassion, and hope. Our time of refreshing can lead to a life so bright with God's likeness that we become the refreshing others need, and the light that points searching hearts to Him.

FATHER, HELP ME BE MINDFUL OF SPENDING TIME IN YOUR PRESENCE, SO I'LL BE REFRESHED AND READY TO BE LIKE YOU.

PAUSE THE CHAOS

You answer us with awesome and righteous deeds, God our Savior,
the hope of all the ends of the earth and of the farthest seas,
Who formed the mountains by Your power.

PSALM 65:5–6 NIV

Those who have climbed a mountain know the irreplaceable gifts in the accomplishment. The tranquility and calm at different stages of the challenge nourish the soul in a way no other experience can. And much like standing at the ocean, standing on top of a mountain gives us an appreciation of how small we are, while magnifying how great God is. It's beautifully humbling.

Nature is God's answer to so many things. Jesus encouraged us to watch the birds and consider the wildflowers if we ever question God's attentiveness to our needs and His faithfulness in meeting them. He put a promise in every rainbow and new mercy in every sunrise. He numbers the stars and calls them by name, orders the seasons, and holds the oceans in place. Is it any wonder we feel at peace in the natural world?

We need time to nurture peace in our lives. Being surrounded by God's handiwork feels like a pause in the chaos to relax with Him for a while. Every living thing is filled with His glory, and when we stop to notice and appreciate His creation, we get a renewed sense of how completely wonderful He is. Everything on this earth lives, moves, and has its being in Him, and He's aware of it all to the point of knowing when a sparrow falls.

Not a single part of our lives is overlooked. God is in every detail of our day and every facet of our future. He can be trusted with every outcome because His love outweighs every obstacle. He wants us to have peace, inside and out, and staying close to Him is how we get it. Go outside today to marvel at His presence in every living thing and appreciate the soothing peace it brings.

DEAR GOD, YOUR PRESENCE IN NATURE HELPS ME NURTURE THE PEACE I NEED. I KNOW YOU SEE EVERY DETAIL OF MY LIFE, AND I TRUST YOU WITH EVERY CARE I HAVE. THANK YOU FOR BEING MY CONSTANT COMFORT.

REST ASSURED

Let us draw near with a true heart in full assurance of faith,
having our hearts sprinkled from an evil conscience
and our bodies washed with pure water.

HEBREWS 10:22 NKJV

No old-time hymnal would be complete without the contributions of Fanny Crosby, who was known as "the Queen of Gospel Songwriters." Despite her blindness, Crosby wrote over eight hundred songs, many of which are still sung today. One of her most popular compositions was "Blessed Assurance." Its lyrics declare:

Blessed assurance, Jesus is mine!

Oh, what a foretaste of glory divine!

Heir of salvation, purchase of God

Born of His Spirit, washed in His blood

This is my story, this is my song

Praising my Savior all the day long

Life was far from perfect for Ms. Crosby. But she understood the power of faith, trusting God and praising Him through thick and thin. When faced with setbacks that might have embittered a lesser woman, Ms. Crosby trusted God's promises and gratefully accepted His plan for her life. She recognized that the peace of God transcends every situation, and we must do the same. We get to walk in the peace and joy of the kingdom of God, showing the world that following the Lord is so worth it.

Do you trust in the ultimate goodness of God's plan for you? Will you face today's challenges with optimism and hope?

Today, as you live in the present and look to the future, remember that God is your Shepherd, now and forever. When you do, you can rest assured that this day, like every other, is only a foretaste of glory divine.

DEAR LORD, THANK YOU FOR THE BLESSED ASSURANCE OF YOUR SALVATION, HOPE, AND JOY. LEAD ME TO WALK IN THOSE THINGS EVERY DAY, SHINING BRIGHT FOR YOU.

HOW TO BE STILL

"Be still, and know that I am God."

PSALM 46:10 NIV

Psalm 46:10 reminds us that God is never asking us to perform for Him or try to be more than we are. He's simply calling us to be still and remember who He is to us. This simple truth can set the tone for everything else in our lives. But it's easy to forget that the knowing part of that verse comes only after the being still part. First, we are invited to enter stillness. Only then can we "know" as we become deeply aware of His comforting presence. And for this to happen, we have to do something that can be challenging for many of us: we have to step away from all our doing and spend some intentional time simply being.

If you've ever tried practicing stillness—whether to pray and hear from God or to reflect on His Word—you may have learned that it can be really tough to stop and pause. It's hard for many of us to sit with ourselves and our thoughts for very long. Once we turn off the screens and other distractions around us and still our bodies, we become keenly aware of how often our minds overthink and how our thought cycles and obsessions function like hamsters on a wheel. Many of us can only take a few minutes of that total stillness and silence before we reach for something to distract us. Learning to be present in the moment is an exercise for the spirit, just as a workout is for the physical body. We may have to ease into it to build those inner muscles, but the longer we are able to settle into that simple awareness, the more of God's wonderful peace we can feel.

LORD, SITTING STILL IS SO ANTI-CULTURAL TODAY. BUT I WANT TO BE QUIET BEFORE YOU AND HEAR YOUR VOICE. PLEASE QUIET MY SPIRIT AND LEAD ME ON.

ISSUES THAT REQUIRE TISSUES

In him we live and move and have our being. . . .
For we are indeed his offspring.

ACTS 17:28 ESV

"If it was a snake, it would have bit you!" A man can stand at the open refrigerator door asking his wife where the butter is, yet be staring right at it. Some people are better at finding things than others. What makes them better? They look in the places others don't think to look.

When you've been through the wringer and feel like God has left you all alone, where do you look when you're trying to find Him? Most would begin their search by reading the Bible or sinking to their knees in prayer. Those are the obvious starting points. But there is misunderstanding at the root of your search if you believe that God truly left you at the point that you needed Him most. If you're looking for God, the good news is you don't have far to go. God never left you at all. In fact, He promised He would never leave us or forsake us (Hebrews 13:5). God has promised to be with us in every moment, good or bad. He is our Shepherd, our Partner, our Guide and Counselor and Friend.

Is God in the middle of your situation or circumstance? Is God in the middle of your personal storm? Is He with you in the middle of your addiction? With you in the midst of your life-changing diagnosis? With you in your grief? Your lawsuit? Your loneliness? Your loss? There are people who see God as distant and detached from the affairs of humanity. However, if that were so, He would not desire to dwell in our hearts.

LORD, THANK YOU FOR BEING CLOSE. MAY ANYONE WHO LOOKS SEE YOU AT THE CENTER OF MY LIFE.

JUMP IN

The eternal God is your refuge,
and underneath are the everlasting arms.

DEUTERONOMY 33:27 NIV

The toddler stood precariously near the edge of the pool, wistfully looking at her father just a few feet away. His arms outstretched, he beckoned his child to jump into his arms. Eyes darted from father to the ever-so-deep water in which he stood. One miscalculation and she might drown, she worried. Growing desperate, she reached out her own arms, leaning forward, hoping he would pick her up off the edge. But it wasn't his plan. Instead, he called her by name. Encouraged her to trust him. And then he patiently waited . . . until she jumped straight into his arms. Heart beating wildly, the little girl found herself instantly against his chest. The waters around her were indeed deep, but he was taller, stronger. She was safe and warm, right where she wanted to be.

As one observing the situation, it's easy to understand the girl's fears, but also the father's heart. Though she felt her world was on the brink of extinction, he knew far better. He was teaching her to trust. And so it is when God calls us to Himself. Though our trials in life seem inevitably devastating, He invites us to trust and jump into His arms. He is not satisfied with simple, half-hearted assent or theoretical trust. He wants full heart, mind, and body thrust with complete abandon into His reliable grace and goodness.

When we finally leap, we find there is no place better than His warm and certain embrace. Today, which areas in your life are keeping you sidelined on the edge of full trust? Talk to God in prayer and take a leap into His loving arms. Discover the place of peace, where you've always wanted to be.

FATHER, YOUR HEART FOR ME IS FULL OF LOVE AND THE DESIRE FOR MY VERY BEST. YOU SEE THAT BETTER THAN I DO. TODAY, I RECOMMIT TO TRUSTING YOUR HEART FOR ME. I WILL LEAP INTO YOUR ARMS.

ALL THESE THINGS

But seek ye first
the kingdom of God, and His righteousness;
and all these things shall be added unto you.

MATTHEW 6:33 KJV

When God came to Solomon in a dream and asked him what he wanted, Solomon could have asked for riches, or wealth, or honor, or the lives of his enemies, or long life for himself (II Chronicles 1:7–11). But instead of asking for worldly things, King Solomon asked God for wisdom and knowledge to help him rule his people. Solomon's request pleased God, so the Father not only gave King Solomon what he asked for, but He gave him everything else as well.

Solomon's kingdom was unrivaled in the ancient world, and Solomon himself bore the fruit of every type of excellence. Which is what captivated the Queen of Sheba, who traveled over fifteen hundred miles to see for herself this wise man of God she had heard so much about.

There is a King greater than Solomon who was born into this world. Jesus Christ, the King of all kings, who gave His life for us to inherit eternal life. The Queen of Sheba came from the uttermost parts of the earth just to hear the wisdom of an earthly king, yet the only distance we have to travel to meet God Himself is from our knees to the floor. We have access to infinite wisdom. What's more, the Bible says that if we ask for wisdom, He promises to give it! There is nothing we need that we lack.

LORD, THANK YOU FOR YOUR PROMISE TO MEET MY EVERY NEED AS I SEEK YOU. THANK YOU FOR PROMISING TO BE FOUND BY THOSE WHO LOOK. I TRUST YOU FOR MY EVERY NEED.

THE SPOT NEXT TO YOU

Give all your worries and cares to God,
for He cares about you.

I PETER 5:7 NLT

Linda arrived home after a long, hard day at work. She swallowed down the burger and fries she'd picked up at the fast-food place, then plopped down on the sofa and put her feet up. Her Jack Russell terrier, Jax, decided to join her. He jumped up onto the sofa and took the spot next to her.

He didn't say a word. (Obviously.) She didn't say a word. They just sat together, enjoying the silence that hovered in the air between them. Linda eventually reached for the remote control and flipped on the television. She wasn't particularly interested in the show she chose but kept the TV playing in the background while she petted Jax and lost herself to her thoughts.

Before long, the cares of the day began to subside. The soothing motion of stroking the pup had a calming effect on her. In fact, Linda began to wonder how her friends who weren't dog owners managed to get through their rough patches without the help of a canine. After an hour or two of resting with the pup at her side, Linda got so relaxed that she almost dozed off.

In many ways, that's how God calms us down. He takes His position right next to us. His very presence is soothing, confirming. He gently eases away the tensions of the day until we are relaxed and still.

No matter what you're going through today, give your worries and cares to the Lord. Allow Him to get close enough to calm you. He has your best interests at heart and wants nothing more to offer a comforting touch.

LORD, I'LL SAVE YOU THE BEST SEAT, RIGHT NEXT TO ME. YOU'RE THE ONLY ONE WHO CAN TRULY RID ME OF THE STRESSES OF THE DAY. YOU COMFORT ME, EVEN WHEN I'M WOUND UP OVER A PROBLEM AT WORK OR A RELATIONAL ISSUE. PRAISE YOU, FATHER, FOR YOUR GENTLE CARE.

PARING DOWN TO SIMPLY LOVE

Don't complicate your lives unnecessarily. Keep it simple.

I CORINTHIANS 7:29 THE MESSAGE

One of the greatest things about camping is being forced to pare down our lives, if only for a few days, to what we absolutely need. And the best part of the adventure is ending the day around a campfire. Camping removes what matters least so we can see, by the light and warmth of a fire, who matters most. It's a perfect reminder that God created our hearts to be fulfilled by whom we love, never what we love.

Are there things complicating our lives unnecessarily? Are we stressing about something we can't change? Do we have a list of to-dos that don't really need a deadline? What's distracting or detouring us from spending our time with the ones we love most—or loving those who need it most? In I Timothy 2:2 we're urged to pray for everyone, including all those in authority, so that "we may live peaceful and quiet lives in all godliness and holiness" (NIV). God chose each of us to be there for one another—in prayer and in presence. Whatever it takes to pare down the busyness of our days for the ones we love is worth doing.

We can only live peaceful, quiet lives one day at a time. We can only put things that matter most in their proper place one step at a time. Maybe there's a part of our busy schedule we can rearrange in order to move love into first place. Maybe there's something that can wait so we can shift our attention to a person rather than a project. Maybe having godliness and holiness is taking time to listen to the brokenhearted. It doesn't take a lot—it only takes a decision to put love in its proper place a little more often every day.

DEAR FATHER, SHOW ME HOW TO SIMPLIFY MY LIFE IN WAYS HONORING YOU AND PREFERRING OTHERS. GIVE ME A HEART READY TO LOVE FIRST AND LET GO OF THE LESSER THINGS.

TRUE REST

Truly my soul finds rest in God.

PSALM 62:1 NIV

Ocean and horizon are like trust and rest. Inseparable. If we don't learn to trust God, we won't experience true rest. Rest is a constant craving of our hearts, in the moments of our hardest days, in the weeks of our longest waits, in the months that bring more questions than answers. When we trust God, we are teaching our souls to rest in Him no matter what happens. He's here, and He sees. What we need. Where we're going. When is best. In the same way there's a steady, refreshing breeze at the ocean's edge, there's a steadfast, reassuring purpose at the heart of God's plan for our lives. Trust and rest come by believing His plans for us are always driven by perfect love.

How do we keep our face toward our purpose and the love guiding it? We keep our focus on hope as ceaseless as the waves. We keep our confidence in faithfulness as sure as the sunrise. We keep our prayers grateful for God's goodness and honest for our growth. He knows us and sees us with cloudless clarity. That should inspire us to trust Him with fearless courage. When we move through our days brave and hopeful, our souls find rest in a world that's fighting to reel our minds and spirits in the opposite direction. Trusting God is the divine tug that will win us the battle.

FATHER, I TRUST YOU WITH MY CARES, MY DAY, AND MY JOURNEY. EVERY HOPE I HAVE IS IN YOUR PERFECT LOVE, THE ONLY PLACE MY SOUL FINDS PERFECT REST.

Today is another chance to remind ourselves that we need to give it all to God. He'll take it all in one fell swoop of love, leaving in its place a lighter spirit, a brighter hope, and a deeper trust. The rest that follows will be like sunshine to our souls and as soothing as sand between our toes.

PRICELESS REST

"Is anyone thirsty?
Come and drink—even if you have no money!
Come, take your choice of wine or milk—it's all free!"

ISAIAH 55:1 NLT

Last month it was your turn. Your daughter got married, and you pulled out all the stops to make it a wonderful memory. But the detailed planning and provision for the large event took quite a toll on your savings. *So much for retiring early,* you thought.

But today is different. You've been invited to someone else's party, and you don't have to prepare a thing. Upon arrival, you notice tables filled to overflowing with every kind of treat imaginable, with drinks all free for the taking, as well. It doesn't take long for you to settle in, surround yourself with friends, and splurge on all the free goodness provided for you!

So, guess what it's going to be like in heaven? The God of all creation has prepared a wedding feast for His people like no other party on our planet. Everything we could wish for and then some will be provided at no cost to us—at all!

But God's celebration over His people doesn't start at some future time. It begins the very moment we decide to accept His invitation to come to Him. At no cost to us, God provides a feast of divine riches that are all ours for the taking because of our connection to Jesus. Are you out of wisdom? He's got that. Could you use a little joy? There's a fountain of it right here. Are you craving real and lasting relationship? You've come to the right place. The one thing He asks is that we leave our baggage with Him at the door. He knows just where to dispose of it. He's even got your party clothes covered, courtesy of Jesus, who already paid for it all.

FATHER, I DON'T DESERVE THE ABUNDANCE OF BEING PART OF YOUR FAMILY. IT OVERWHELMS ME TO THINK ABOUT IT! THANK YOU FOR YOUR EXTREME GENEROSITY IN MY LIFE.

GOLDEN GOODNESS

How sweet Your words taste to me;
they are sweeter than honey.

PSALM 119:103 NLT

Would you travel 55,000 miles for a pound of honey? Probably not. But a nest of foraging honeybees would put in that kind of work to produce the sweet treat. Each forager bee leaves the hive daily to collect nectar from at least one hundred flowers before returning home. As they suck out the nectar from each flower, they safely store it in a separate stomach––the one reserved just for honey. With their honey tummies full, they fly back to the hive and deposit their golden goodness into hexagonal-shaped honeycomb chambers, capping them with a layer of wax when full. In this way, they have plenty of food stored up for future seasons when winter looms and blooms are scarce. Altogether, it takes more than five hundred bees visiting more than two million flowers to create one pound of honey.

Would you ever have imagined how much work went into that tiny teaspoon of honey you dab on your toast or swirl in your tea? But put it straight on your tongue and you know it's a true golden treasure, the kind of treat only God could mastermind.

It's no wonder, then, that the psalmist compares God's Word to the sweetness of honey. The Bible you hold in your hands is no ordinary book. It is a miracle of God, the single sweet message of saving grace spoken by God through the pens of ordinary people through the course of more than a thousand years. His labor of love satisfies our souls in a way no other earthly pleasure ever could. Today, savor the sweetness of God's truth and love, and thank Him for all the extravagant measures He took to bring the truth to your heart.

LORD, TODAY I WILL REVEL IN YOUR SWEETNESS. I AM SO THANKFUL YOUR LOVE IS GENTLE, KIND, AND EASILY WON.

THUNDERS AND WHISPERS

Call to Me, and I will answer you,
and show you great and mighty things,
which you do not know.

JEREMIAH 33:3 NKJV

A lull in the conversation between strangers or acquaintances is often uncomfortable, while conversations with loved ones and close friends are sprinkled with familiar pauses and breaks. But what happens when God is silent, and that silence is more than a pause or a lull? As close as King David felt to the Lord, he wondered at times if God had forsaken him. "O my God, I cry by day, but you do not answer, and by night, but I find no rest" (Psalm 22:2 ESV). There are times in our prayer life and in our earnest conversations with God that He goes unusually silent. Is He distracted or uninterested in hearing us pour our hearts out to Him? Could He be bored? Quite the opposite. The psalmist in 55:16–17 (NIV) says, "As for me, I call to God . . . and He hears my voice." God is listening. He's just not always answering in the way you expect Him to.

God speaks in both thunders and whispers, but in His silence, He speaks much more. Silence is a time for self-reflection, for listening. Lean into the silence. Be still with Him. Ask God to show you if there is a sin you need to come clean about. Is it truly possible for God to be silent if your Bible is right there next to you? If you want to talk to someone, you pick up your phone to call or text. If you want to hear from God, open His Word, the Bible. When you call unto Him, God promises to show you great and mighty things. Our hearts hear God better than our ears.

LORD, I TRUST THAT YOU HEAR MY CALLS AND CRIES. THANK YOU FOR LISTENING. HONE MY EARS AND MY SPIRITUAL SENSES TO CATCH EVEN YOUR GENTLEST WHISPER WHEN YOU SPEAK.

BUSYNESS IS NOT BEST

Return unto thy rest, O my soul;
for the LORD hath dealt bountifully with thee.

PSALM 116:7 KJV

Mary and Martha both loved Jesus. When He came to visit, one of them sat at His feet while the other prepared a meal. It wasn't the fact that Martha cooked that caused problems. It was the fact that she allowed overwhelm and responsibility to be her guides. She did not worship and serve in love; she compared herself to her sister, Mary, and found Mary lacking. Worship can never happen when we're comparing ourselves to others. And busyness, in and of itself, is not a virtue.

For most of us, life is busy, perhaps too busy for our own good. We rush from place to place, with scarcely a moment to spare, checking smartphones along the way. Meanwhile, we're constantly bombarded by a steady stream of media, much of it disturbing. No wonder we're stressed!

Has the busy pace of twenty-first-century life robbed you of the peace and serenity that could otherwise be yours through Jesus Christ? If so, it's time to slow down, do less, and appreciate life a little more.

As you consider your priorities, remember that time with God is paramount. You owe it to yourself to spend time each day with your Creator, seeking His guidance and studying His Word. Those quiet moments of prayer and meditation are invaluable. When you let God help you organize your day, you'll find that He'll give you the time and the tools to do the most important tasks on your to-do list. And what about all those less-important things on your list? Perhaps they're best left undone.

LORD, HELP ME TO KNOW THE RIGHT BALANCE OF WORK AND REST, SERVICE AND RECEIVING, RESPONSIBILITY AND TRUST. YOUR WAYS ARE ALWAYS BEST.

SLOWING DOWN TO SEE THE GOOD STUFF

No doubt about it! God is good. . . .
But I nearly missed it, missed seeing His goodness.

PSALM 73:1–2 THE MESSAGE

We see more when we slow down. When we walk through a neighborhood we've driven through a hundred times, we see details we've never noticed before. Slowing our pace opens our eyes. It's important to slow down—when we make decisions, when our schedules are out of control, and when we feel stress smothering our tranquility.

God is good at teaching us to use the brakes. "Rest in the Lord; wait patiently for Him to act" (Psalm 37:7 TLB). "God wants His loved ones to get their proper rest" (Psalm 127:2 TLB). "Relax and rest. God has showered you with blessings" (Psalm 116:7 THE MESSAGE).

If we keep sprinting through our days, when we finally stop and look back . . . all we'll see is a blur. We'll realize we've missed too much of what was important and worried about too many things that weren't. God knows that rest helps us retain our balance. Slowing down encourages us to see opportunities we're missing to love people, show kindness, and do things that light up the world.

Where we are in our lives, what we do every day, and the people we're here to love are perfectly in place. It's up to us to pace ourselves in a way that values what God has given us. We won't get a day back once it's spent. Slow down and make sure to see every detail of His kindness in your life at this moment. Don't hurry past the good stuff.

DEAR GOD, OPEN MY EYES TO THE PRIORITIES IN MY LIFE. I DON'T WANT TO MISS THE LOVE AND PURPOSE IN THEM. GIVE ME WISDOM IN KEEPING EVERYTHING IN BALANCE SO I INVEST MY TIME IN THE RIGHT PURSUITS AND THE MOST IMPORTANT THINGS.

WORTH THE WAIT

My soul, wait silently for God alone,
for my expectation is from Him.

PSALM 62:5 NKJV

A mother and father waiting for the birth of their child are said to be "expecting." This special time overshadows everything else in their lives. As the baby grows, so does their sense of excitement and anticipation. Average days take on a deeper significance as they wait for that day of jubilation when their child finally arrives. There's never a point when the parents are doubting that they are truly pregnant. The mother's belly grows, and eventually she feels kicks. Ultrasounds evoke images of tiny bones, toes, a heartbeat, and the occasional sucking of a thumb. And due to centuries of experience, they know how pregnancy works: there will be a child at the right time.

Now, this is a broken world, and there are times when a pregnancy ends before birth, and we weep. But we do know according to Scripture that a child is a child even before he or she reaches the womb. We have every reason to believe that any child, from the womb and beyond, is a soul bound for heaven.

Life is always worth rejoicing in. And pregnancy is a beautiful metaphor for God's presence in our lives. With the Holy Spirit, we have every reason to live a life of expectation, as well. We should wake each morning eager to see what the day will bring, how God's goodness will play out for us. Without Him, we have only the promise that our bodies will become older and weaker. But with Him, life becomes "eternal life," with all His joyous promises spread out before us. If you are a Jesus follower, you have every reason to expect to see good things. Wait for them, anticipate them, prepare for them. Keep your eyes open. Your days are certain to take on deeper significance as you await that day of jubilation when you finally see your God face-to-face.

LORD GOD, THIS IS YOUR WORLD, AND I AM YOUR CHILD. I EAGERLY EXPECT YOUR GOODNESS. THANK YOU FOR LOVING ME SO RELIABLY AND COMPLETELY. AMEN.

Dear Friend,

This book was prayerfully crafted with you, the reader, in mind. Every word, every sentence, every page was thoughtfully written, designed, and packaged to encourage you—right where you are this very moment. At DaySpring, our vision is to see every person experience the life-changing message of God's love. So, as we worked through rough drafts, design changes, edits, and details, we prayed for you to deeply experience His unfailing love, indescribable peace, and pure joy. It is our sincere hope that through these Truth-filled pages your heart will be blessed, knowing that God cares about you—your desires and disappointments, your challenges and dreams.

He knows. He cares. He loves you unconditionally.

BLESSINGS!
THE DAYSPRING BOOK TEAM

Additional copies of this book and
other DaySpring titles can be purchased
at fine retailers everywhere.
Order online at <u>dayspring.com</u>
or
by phone at 1-877-751-4347